# TASSELS, TIEBACKS & TRIMMINGS

## *and how to use them*

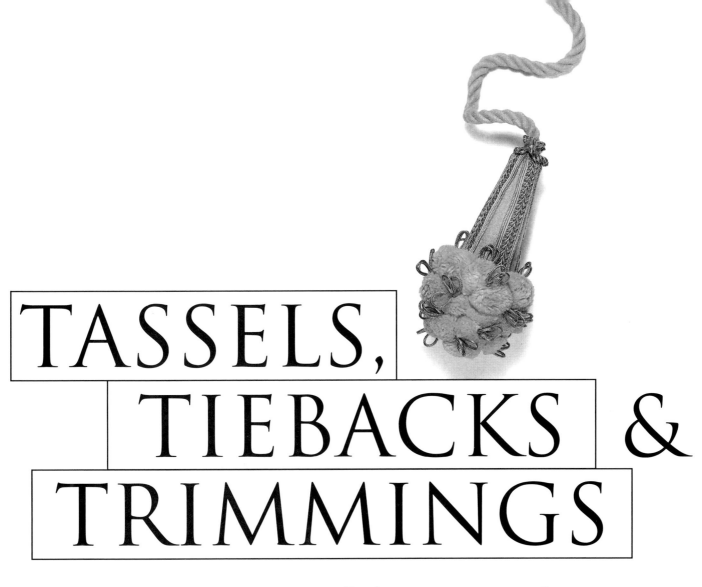

# TASSELS, TIEBACKS & TRIMMINGS

*and how to use them*

ELIZABETH VALENTI

Chilton Book Company
Radnor, Pennsylvania

A Quarto Book

Copyright © 1997 Quarto Inc

ISBN 0-8019-8937-X

A CIP record for this book is available from the
Library of Congress

*This book was designed and produced by*
Quarto Publishing plc
The Old Brewery, 6 Blundell Street
London N7 9BH

*Senior editor* Michelle Pickering
*Senior art editor* Catherine Shearman
*Designer* Debbie Mole
*Illustrators* Terry Evans, Elsa Godfrey, Nicola Gregory
*Photographers* Hannah Lewis, Anna Hodgson
*Text editor* Susie Ward
*Editorial assistant* Judith Evans
*Picture research manager* Giulia Hetherington
*Art director* Moira Clinch

*Typeset by* Central Southern Typesetters,
Eastbourne, UK
*Manufactured by* Eray Scan Pte Ltd, Singapore
*Printed by* Star Standard Industries (Pte) Ltd, Singapore

# contents

# INTRODUCTION

My interest in tassels and trimmings began many years ago during visits to Paris and the nearby chateaux of Versailles and Malmaison, and later to the chateaux of the Loire Valley. Some of the more well known chateaux could be very crowded and often the guide would speak only in French. Therefore, if I found myself pressed close to a huge window, my attention would wander from the history of the castle, the family, the paintings and the porcelain to a close inspection of what was nearest to me. I became very involved with observations of fixtures and fittings, of finishes, edges, borders, ropes, braids, and perhaps most of all, tassels. These delightful objects would often be fragile and in urgent need of repair, but their intrinsic beauty and complexity, coupled with the stunning combinations of color and texture, were still there to admire.

Anyone who focuses on a particular specialization probably has no idea at the outset of the wealth of information and interest that awaits them. What starts as a passing intrigue can soon become a passion, with the desire to know more leading one in a host of different directions. I was hooked by these delightful embellishments. I was amused that they were at once so fascinating and yet served no really useful purpose. They are a reflection of caprice, of fashion and personal taste. There is no right or wrong way to use them; they can be restrained and minimal, or madly over the top and self-indulgent.

Tassels are made from molds, originally wooden, which can be carved or turned into a vast variety of shapes. Each type of mold has its own name, which is often reminiscent of the shapes of pastries or fruits – for example, pain de sucre, macaroon, gourde, olive and poire. They can be three-dimensional or flat, and shaped like arrows, domes, bells or balls. Each particular style has its own name, which indicates fashions of past times, such as personalities, songs, dances and other interests. They include polonaises, papillon, postillonnée, napolitaine, jasmin and duchess, to name but a very few. A classic tassel comprises a neck, mold and skirt, although there are many variations within these constraints.

It is essentially the French who perfected the art of tassel-making. Initially – and to a great extent today – the production of tassels and trimmings

*La Passementière, from* Journal la Caricature, *was published around 1830 as part of a series of illustrations showing the costumes worn by various merchants.*

was in the hands, literally, of artisans. These makers were always apart from the general making of textiles, being specialists in their own right. As early as medieval times, ribbon weavers and braid makers were involved in the decoration of ecclesiastical robes and furnishings, military and ceremonial wear, as well as decorations for domestic use by the wealthy. It was during the seventeenth century, when Louis XIV began building the Palais de Versailles, that the business of trimmings entered the height of its success. Sixteen fifty-three saw the foundation of a guild especially for the purpose of making *passementerie* (decorative trimming). The taste for flamboyance and the showing off of wealth provided opportunities galore for the passementiers. With the importation of silks, velvets and brocades from Italy and the Middle East, this marked a time of prolific imagination for the trimmings makers. Their tassels were exquisitely detailed; the creativity was breathtaking.

*Tassels come in all sorts of shapes and sizes. History has handed down numerous forms of inspiration, from as far afield as Africa, Asia and the courts of Europe. The modern tassels shown on these pages exemplify the beauty of design and meticulous detail that can still be found.*

By the mid-eighteenth century, there were around 550 passementiers working in Paris; by the end of the nineteenth century, this number had reduced to around sixty. The French and Industrial Revolutions had both taken their toll. Under the reign of Louis Philippe, however, there came a new kind of prosperity. Power-driven machinery changed the approach to manufacture; Egyptian cotton was cheaper and more easily available than silk. And there was now a new clientele: the expanding bourgeoisie. It was no longer only the kings and aristocracy who had access to such decorative riches. The new industrialists wanted to show off their wealth too. Decoration became elaborate and rich once again, and the finished articles now had a more regular, manufactured look compared to those of the previous era.

The Victorian and Edwardian eras followed, epitomized by rich decoration. Rooms were cluttered with dressed-to-kill sofas and chairs, mantlepieces and sideboards, pillows and curtains. Floor-sweeping bullion fringes, tasseled picture hangers and bobble-trimmed piano stools were everywhere to be seen. Art Nouveau and Art Deco followed, featuring new discoveries in chemical dyes and artificial fibers, as well as the use of plastic as an accessory. Then came the Second World War, distracting people from their previous frivolity. By the 1960's, the once glorious population of Parisian passementiers had dwindled to around twenty. These were mainly family-run businesses, which continued to combine machine and handcrafting techniques. Nowadays, the number is even smaller.

However, with the second millenium coming upon us, a renewed interest in tassels and trimmings has emerged, alongside a surge of interest in home crafting. This may be a reaction to mass-production, to the "sameness" of

everything, to feeling a loss of personal identity. We are now used to the chain store and the shopping mall. Very few people have to make anything from scratch if they do not want to or have not the time, be it making clothes or making meals. Therefore, "making" has become the new leisure/pleasure industry. It provides real personal satisfaction with something tangible to show for one's efforts that perhaps, for some of us, our jobs no longer offer. Craft courses offering hands-on guidance are flourishing. Good quality, professionally run craft fairs show ample evidence of people's success. However, there is no need to eschew everything machine-made in favor of the home crafted; perhaps the two apparently diverse approaches can go hand-in-hand, just as they did in centuries past. This is certainly my belief. Individuals recognize and long for quality as well as a pride in self-achievement. I believe that, despite dismal cries to the contrary, we are not losing our skills and that new materials and techniques, together with a good look at what has been achieved in the past, will provide a promising future full of quality and individualism.

So, on the next occasion that you find yourself in a cathedral, historical house or museum, enjoy the history and the overall ambience. But also remember to look at the detail, the particular. You might find it could well change the course of your life.

*This painting from the Musée de Versailles shows Empress Marie-Louise of France, the wife of Napoleon I, amid the glorious decor of their palace. Note the plentiful use of gold trimmings and tassels, typical of the era.*

## Tassels around the World

The desire to decorate family, home and animals is evident in numerous countries around the world. The tassel and similar trimmings play an important part in the scheme of decoration, and there are numerous examples of their use: to denote tribal identity, power, wealth, ritual, ceremony, religion, etc. Tassels are made by tribal peoples, nomads, peasants, farmers and villagers from whatever materials are readily available. They might use grasses, hair, wool, skin, bone, vegetation, shells, feathers, etc., to produce examples that range from the beautiful to the bizarre.

North American Indians use horsehair to make long ragged tassels for their garments, and cut into the skins of their tunics to make fringed finishes. In Africa, the Asante sword bearers wear fringed wrist and ankle decorations in real gold, and scalloped gold headdresses. In Peru, llamas wear tassels in their ears for identification. Guatemalan textiles are brilliantly colored, woven and embroidered cottons and wools, and tassels and huge bobbles are used to trim striped fabric garments, twisted braid headbands and soft fabric bags.

In China, the mountainside Miao tribe trim their children's hats with bobbles and their baby bags with tassels hanging from appliquéed coins. In Japan, there is a long history of the use of tassels. During the era of the samurai warriors, tassels and elaborate decoration were a distinctive feature. Armor and weaponry often had numerous forms of embellishment, with tassels made of paper, horsehair and other materials. Tassels still feature heavily in Japanese decoration, particularly at special festivals.

In Europe, horse harnesses are often trimmed with tassels in bright colors for festive occasions, and in black for funerals. Trucks are decorated with them in Afghanistan, and rickshaws in China. Robes worn by modern-day ecclesiasts still feature tassels as a symbol of power. Graduates attending their degree ceremonies wear flat caps decorated with a single tassel. The tassel is moved from one side of the cap to the other upon receiving their certificate.

The examples are endless and the love of this delightful ephemera continues to be as strong today. Tassels feature on modern shoes, handbags, hats, jewelry, on the seams of stockings, as well as the many uses in the home. The uses for this "useless" embellishment are myriad.

*Left: The tassels used on this Chinese silk bag feature elaborate knots and metallic threads.*
*Above left: These two strings of multiple tassels are decorative animal trappings from the East.*
*Above right: This tassel-bedecked man is a Moroccan waterman.*

## STYLE GUIDE

There are eight design themes in this book. It is not necessary to find exact copies of the tassels and trimmings used in the projects, merely to find ones that suit the overall theme.

### ETHNIC

This look is inspired by the textiles and art of tribal peoples as far afield as Africa, Afghanistan and Guatemala. Colors should be bold and fabrics natural. Patterns can be big, bold stripes, ikat weaves, or a set of repeating patterns in a variety of sizes. Tassels, fringes and shaped edges, such as zig-zags, form an essential part of finishing off raw edges. Visit craft fairs, museums, libraries and bookstores for inspiration, and whenever you go on vacation, take notice of any local forms of decoration. Buy anything that you like and can afford, even if you do not know what to use it for at the time — inspiration can come later!

### CLASSICAL

The inspiration for this look is the classical architecture of Greece and Rome, with their great stone pillars and decorative capitals. It conjures up an age

of elegance, but also of simplicity. In the West, this approach to architecture has been copied over and over again in public buildings, such as libraries, museums, churches and government centers. Echo the color of stone and marble, and look at the details on artefacts such as Greek pots and jewelry for inspiration. Spirals and scrolls feature frequently.

## COOL CALICOES

The inspiration for this look comes from our pioneer days, from the founding of America. Think about what we know from photo archive material and early films showing what they would have worn. The look is unpretentious, clean and laundry-fresh. It combines basic block-printed florals and woven checks, as well as the blues and whites of transfer-printed china and lace. You can transfer this look to your home quite easily. It can be a tremendous relief after complicated and rich color schemes to relax with a simple, basic look.

## FRENCH

For this look think about Louis XIV, the Sun King, and work backward. Think about richness, sophistication of design, elegance and over-the-top decor. Think about Versailles and lashings of gold. Trim every edge with it. If you cannot get gold, then ocher chenille or similar will do. You might find a wonderful piece of old velvet or brocade in a thrift store that you can trim and revitalize. If modern tapestries, which can be expensive, are out of your reach, then choose some print ones. There are some good ones available, and if you choose muted colors, you should be successful.

## FABULOUS FLORA

There are many examples of the use of natural forms in pattern-making, but surely the most popular and enduring is that of the flower. Its infinite variety offers the designer a range of possibilities from the simplest sprig or single flower to the most sophisticated intertwinings of stem and branch. They were used in the furnishings of the emperors of China, and the early American settlers, when they started to make money, depicted their status with stenciled flowers on their walls, painted by traveling stencilers. The range available in today's stores is wide enough to suit everyone's tastes.

## RUSTIC

This look is inspired by get-away-from-it-all simplicity. It echoes the back-to-basics ethos, with the less-is-more theme as a strong feature. Forget traditional ways of using trimmings and fabrics. Instead, go for simple but functional ideas, with the trimmings inspired by a visit to a ship's chandlers or the agricultural section of a museum. Use inexpensive fabric such as linen and muslin. Detail should have a slightly utilitarian feel, with features using ropes or braided and knotted string. This look is best teamed with the right kind of background, such as flagstone floors, terracotta tiles and rush matting.

## MEDIEVAL

This is a look characterized by the architecture and furnishings of the great cathedrals of Europe. Rich, dark and heavy brocades and velvets from Italy and the Middle East were used, and ecclesiastical robes were decorated with embroideries and braids depicting the importance of the wearer. Thick door draperies kept out draughts and huge dark tassels glinting with gold or silver bullion held back the fullness. It is possible to buy similar modern versions of the fabrics from specialist ecclesiastical suppliers but these are not cheap. However, by painting walls in rich, dark, strong colors, and using fabrics to tone, you can begin to achieve the ambience. Buy lots of big church candles and you are well on your way.

## TARTANS & CHECKS

Tartan is a checked cloth whose patterns and colors were used to denote a particular clan membership in the Highlands of Scotland. The Scottish kilt is probably its most well known use. Tartan was introduced into the home by the Victorians, who loved its combination of opulence, respectability and formality. A similar sort of multi-colored check is produced in India called a Madras check. America has always been a country of check lovers, being wearers of simple checks since pioneer days.

*This biblical painting* dating from the late-medieval period shows a variety of tassels and trimmings, used both on the tents and as part of people's attire.

# MATERIALS & EQUIPMENT

*A tape measure, sharp pair of scissors, dressmaking pins, pencil or tailor's chalk, and a range of sewing threads and needles suitable for the fabrics and colors you are using are the only essential items. You may also need curtain heading tape, hooks, rings, hanging clips, grommets and grommet punch, all of which are easy to find.*

# stitch directory

The stitches shown here include everything you will need to make the projects in this book, but feel free to adapt them and to use others if you prefer. Many different stitches and sewing techniques are suitable for use with tassels and trimmings. What you choose to use will depend on the project you are making and the type of trimming you are using. You may find yourself trying to sew some quite unusual shaped tassels and trimmings to your soft furnishings, so a certain amount of adaptability will be necessary. However, you will soon learn which techniques you prefer to use and which ones produce the best results for you.

### hand stitches

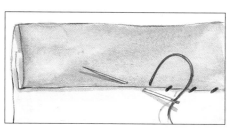

**Slip-stitch**

This is used for hemming lightweight fabrics, as the stitches should be virtually invisible on the right side. Pick up a few threads from the back of the fabric and then stitch through the folded edge. Slip-stitch is also useful for sewing braid invisibly to the front of fabric. For this, only pick up threads from behind the braid and then from the fabric under it.

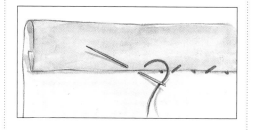

**Hem stitch**

Use this to hem medium-weight fabrics and to hold down loose folds and edges. Pick up the threads on both layers of fabric and then pull the needle through.

**Herringbone stitch**

Use this stitch to secure hems on heavy fabrics. The stitches should cross over each other at top and bottom.

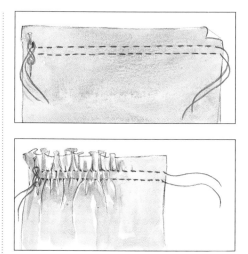

**Gathering stitch**

Sew two rows of long, straight stitches close together. Anchor around a pin at one end and then pull up the threads to gather. Distribute the fabric evenly.

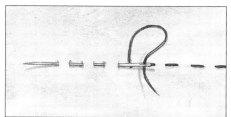

**Basting stitch**

Sew a row of long, straight stitches to join pieces of fabric, etc., temporarily.

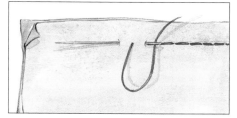

**Backstitch**

This is a strong stitch, comparable to a machine straight stitch. Two or three back stitches on top of each other can also be used to finish off hand sewing.

## *machine stitches*

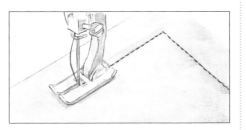

### Straight stitch
This forms a thin, solid line and is used for seams and for sewing braid to fabric. Sometimes it is sewn on the right side of fabric, to sew items together decoratively, when it may be called top-stitch.

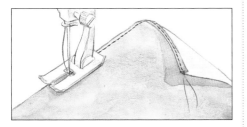

### Edge stitch
This is straight stitch sewn at the edge of fabric. It is usually used for hems. Line up the inside or outside edge of the presser foot with the edge of the fabric to maintain a straight line.

### Zig-zag stitch
This is used as a decorative stitch, when the zig-zags can be any size required. It is also used to appliqué insets, such as lace, onto fabric, as it joins the pieces and finishes off the raw edges at the same time. It is also used to make buttonholes.

## *stitching techniques*

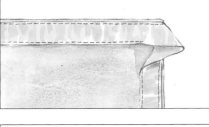

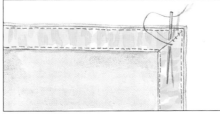

### Mitering
Straight stitch all along both sides of the braid or fabric strip as far as the first corner. Pin the braid/fabric along the next edge. Fold in the corner to make a neat, diagonal line. Secure the miter with a few tiny hand stitches.

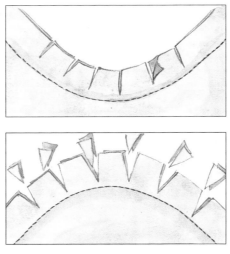

### Notching and clipping seams
When seams are positioned on curves, both inward and outward, they must be notched or clipped to enable the fabric to fit comfortably into the curved shape. Take care not to cut into the stitching.

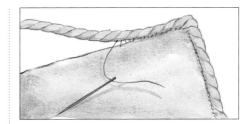

### Stitching rope/cord
Pick up a few threads on the main fabric and then on the underside of the cord, rope, etc. Carry on in a sort of spiral slip-stitch, pulling the stitching taut occasionally as you go.

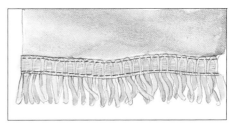

### Stitching fringing
Most fringing is attached to a straight length of braid. If narrow, sew one line of straight stitches; if wide, sew a line of straight stitches along both edges of the braid. Alternatively, sew straight stitches along the edge nearest the fringing and slip-stitch the remaining edge.

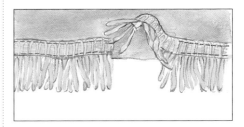

### Neatening ends of braid/fringing
If the two ends of braid meet, turn under a small amount on one piece, and lay this on top of the raw end of the other piece. Hand sew across the width of the braid. If they do not meet, turn under both ends and sew across each one.

# ETHNIC

Natural fabrics with an irregular weave, such as woven blankets and handspun woolen yarns, are ideal. Juxtapose bold stripes and patterns with trimmings in vibrant colors — cochineal red, indigo and green.

# fringed blanket

*Blankets look best if they are simply hung at the window, with minimum preparation but maximum effect. Metal hanging hooks can be inserted directly into the blanket. A matching tie-back can be added or the curtain can be left to hang loosely in folds.*

## MATERIALS

◆ Striped blanket or similar fabric

◆ Hooks and curtain rings

◆ Brass rings for tie-back (optional)

### CURTAIN – MEASURING UP

Use a blanket with either blanket-stitched edges or with fringes. If necessary, sew pieces together to achieve the desired width. The curtain needs to be the width of the pole plus an extra allowance so that it hangs in folds. On average, 8 to 12 hooks will be adequate for each curtain, depending on the weight of the blanket.

**I. Fold one of the stitched or fringed** edges of the blanket over so that it falls to the front of the curtain. Make sure that the folded section is even along its length. Distribute the metal hooks along the folded edge, making sure that they pierce about ½in (12mm) of fabric so that the blanket is held securely. Attach the hooks to the curtain rings and hang above the window.

### TIE-BACK – MEASURING UP

Loop a tape measure around the curtain at the desired height, holding the ends against the wall where the tie-back will be fixed. This gives the length of the tie-back. The width should be around 4in (10cm). Add ⅝in (1.5cm) for hems.

**I. Cut a strip of blanket to the length** and width required. Thick fabric does not need to be stiffened, so simply turn over all the edges to the wrong side by ⅝in (1.5cm). Slip-stitch in place. Sew a brass ring to each end of the tie-back and loop over a brass hook on the wall.

# pom-pom cords

*This method of hanging a curtain is simple, speedy and decorative. Grommets are easily punched into most fabrics and should not need heading tape. Choose a colorful cord and decorate each end with beads and pom-poms.*

## MATERIALS

◆ Striped blanket or similar fabric

◆ Large grommets and grommet punch

◆ Cord

◆ Pom-poms and beads

CURTAIN – MEASURING UP
The cord should be approximately three times the width of the curtain. You will need two pom-poms for each end of the cord and as many beads as desired.

1. If using a blanket with fringed ends, turn over the top edge by about 3in (7.5cm) to display the fringes on the right side. Then attach the grommets through both layers, if the fabric is not too thick.

2. If using more conventional fabric, hem the sides by turning over ⅝in (1.5cm) to the wrong side. Press. Repeat and sew. Turn up the bottom hem by 1½in (4cm). Press. Repeat and sew the hem. Turn the top hem by 2in (5cm) to the wrong side and press. Repeat and sew.

3. Attach the grommets, distributing them evenly across the top hem. Pass the cord in a continuous loop through the grommets, working from the front over the top and down through the back.

4. To help organize the distribution of the cord, pin it to the curtain for guidance. Thread some beads onto each end of the cord. Tie each end to the center of a short length of cord. Thread beads onto these and then sew a pom-pom onto each end. Pass the pole through the cord loops. Remove any pins and hang the curtain in place.

5. Alternatively, use a separate loop of cord for each grommet, making sure that each loop is of equal length so that the curtain hangs evenly. Tie each loop with a double knot and attach beads and pom-poms to the ends of the cords.

# stylish stripes

*This simple style works well either as window curtains or hung around a four-poster bed. Choose a fabric with a wide stripe that can be extended to form loops or sew strips of contrasting fabric down the length of the curtain.*

MATERIALS

◆ Fabric for main curtain

◆ Contrasting fabric for stripes, loops, and facing

◆ Fringing

MEASURING UP

Measure the width of the pole and add additional fullness as required. Cut each curtain to the length required, plus 6in (15cm) for hems. Cut a facing strip to the width of the curtain plus 1in (2.5cm), and 3in (8cm) deep. For loops with a finished width of 3in (7.5cm), cut strips 7in (18cm) by 9in (23cm). Adjust according to the width of the stripe you are using. If you intend to sew strips of contrasting fabric down the length of the curtain, cut them to the width desired plus 1¼in (3cm) seam allowances. They must be the length of the curtain plus a hem allowance.

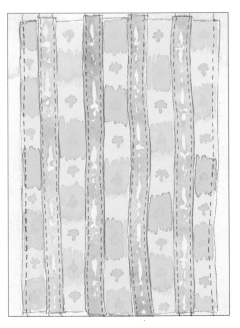

▲ **1. Hem the sides of the curtains.** Turn the fabric to the wrong side by ⅝in (1.5cm) and press. Repeat and sew. If sewing strips of contrasting fabric down the length of the curtain, press the seam allowance of ⅝in (1.5cm) to the wrong side down each long edge. Lay the strips of fabric on the curtain, both fabrics right side up.

▲ **2. Baste each strip in place and top-stitch down both sides.** Remove the basting stitches and press. Turn up the bottom hem by 2in (5cm) and press. Repeat and sew.

**3. Now make the loops. Fold each strip** lengthwise, right sides together. Sew down the length ⅝in (1.5cm) in from the edge. Turn right side out and press. Fold each strip in half to form a loop and sew across the cut edge.

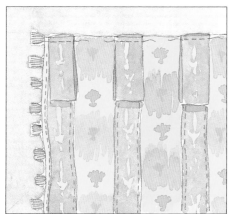

▲ **4. Place the loops along the top edge** of the curtain, right sides together and raw edges even. Line them up with the stripe of the fabric. Baste in place. Sew the tassel fringe down the length of one side hem.

▲ **5. Lay the facing across the top edge** of the curtain, right sides together. Sew through the facing, loops, and main fabric, ⅝in (1.5cm) in from the edge. Remove the basting stitches.

▲ **6. Turn the facing to the wrong side,** turn in the ends to neaten and turn up the lower hem by ⅝in (1.5cm). Sew across the curtain and slip-stitch the sides. Press. Draw the pole through the loops and hang in place.

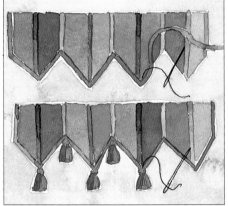

**▲ 2. Blanket material can be cut** straight into and used without lining or backing. Hand-stitch the braid along the zig-zag turnings and on the sides to avoid a "dent" caused by machine stitching. Then stitch individual tassels onto each point of the zig-zag.

# zig-zag valance

*This is a simple, easy-to-make valance which has an unusual hem accentuated by the trim. The valance can also be made with a straight hem, and the trim can be contrasting or multi-colored.*

## MATERIALS

◆ Blanket or similar fabric
◆ Interfacing (if using lightweight fabric)
◆ Braid and tassels
◆ Brass clips

## MEASURING UP

Measure the required width. Decide the overall depth of the valance and the depth of each V shape. Start with a rough idea of the proportions; the paper pattern can always be adjusted.

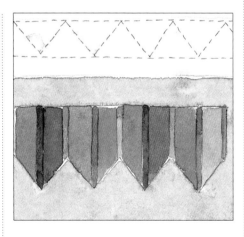

**▲ 1. First, make a paper pattern.** Cut a piece of paper to the width and overall depth of the valance. Draw two parallel lines corresponding to the required depth of the V shapes. Evenly space the V's between the lines. Check the whole look by taping the paper template above the window. Make any adjustments to the shape. When using conventional fabric, add a seam allowance of ⅝in (1.5cm) all around.

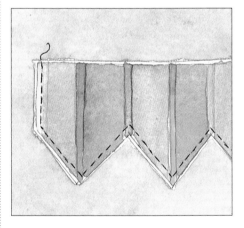

**▲ 3. For more conventional fabric, cut** two pieces of fabric, plus one piece of interfacing without the seam allowances. Place the interfacing on the wrong side of one fabric piece and iron. Put both pieces of fabric right sides together and sew all around, leaving a gap of 6in (15cm). Turn through to the right side and press carefully. Slip-stitch the opening closed. Attach the braid and tassels as described in Step 2.

**4. Distribute the brass clips evenly** along the top of the valance and hang on a brass pole.

# checked wallhanging

*A simple method of adding interest to your walls is to use strongly colored contrasting fabrics as wallhangings. Add more vibrancy to the room by extending the look into a richly colored pillow.*

## MATERIALS

◆ Fabric for central panel

◆ Contrasting fabric for outer squares

◆ Backing fabric, e.g. calico

◆ Grommets and grommet punch

◆ Cord and wooden buttons

◆ 2 poles

## MEASURING UP

Measure the length and width of the hanging in relation to your poles. Work out the proportions of the contrasting fabrics and add seam allowances of ⅝in (1.5cm) to each square and to the central panel. Cut a rectangle of calico large enough to back the entire hanging.

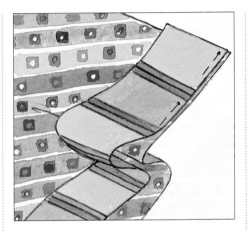

▲ **1. Lay out your pieces of fabric to** check the proportion of color and pattern. Sew the outer squares together using ⅝in (1.5cm) seams. Sew the bands of squares to the main fabric rectangle. Clip the seams, and press them open.

▲ **2. Lay the front of the wallhanging** face down on the rectangle of calico. Sew around all four sides using seam allowances of ⅝in (1.5cm) and leaving a gap of 6in (15cm) on one side.

**3. Turn right side out and slip-stitch** the gap closed. Press. Insert the grommets as desired across the top and bottom edges. Tie the wallhanging to the poles with knotted lengths of cord, threading on wooden buttons if desired.

## PILLOW

Use the same method as the wallhanging to make a pillow. Knot individual wooden buttons to short lengths of cord and sew these into the seams when joining the front and back of the pillow together.

# zig-zag pillow

*This beautiful pillow is made from striped fabric in bright, bold colors. Zig-zag panels decorated with tassels are added to create a striking and colorful feast for the eye.*

## MATERIALS
◆ Fabric with wide stripes
◆ Square pillow form
◆ Zipper
◆ Tassels

## MEASURING UP

Measure the width of the pillow form across the middle and add 1in (2.5cm) to give the length and overall width for the pillow fabric. Subtract the width of two stripes from the overall width of the pillow to calculate the width of the central panel. The zig-zag edging should be as wide as one stripe.

◀ **I. Transfer your measurements to** paper, making a paper pattern for the main fabric in the center, and add two more pattern pieces for each of the contrasting side bands. The three pieces should form a square when sewn together. Make a paper pattern for the zig-zag trim, following the instructions for the zig-zag valance on page 20. Each zig-zag should be the width of a single stripe. Add seam allowances of ⅝in (1.5cm) on all sides of all pattern pieces.

▲ **2. Cut two center rectangles with the** stripes running horizontally across them and four side bands made up of one stripe each. For the back, sew one of the center rectangles to one of the side bands.

Sew the other side of the center rectangle to another band for 2in (5cm) at each end, leaving a gap for the zipper. Baste the gap along the seam lines.

▲ 5. **Lay the two zig-zag strips on the** right side of the remaining center panel, sides aligned and points facing inward. Lay the two outer straight bands on top, right side down, and sew through all layers. Open out and press the zig-zag trim outward.

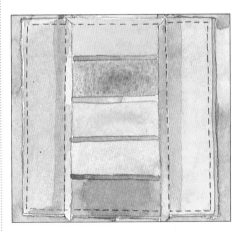

▲ 6. **Place the back and front squares** together, right sides facing. Check that the edges and corners match. Sew around all four sides, ⅝in (1.5cm) from the edge (baste first, if preferred). Clip the corners and turn right side out through the zipper opening. Press. Finally, sew a tassel where each end of the zig-zag trim meets the side seams of the pillow. (This will ensure that the trim always remains facing outward.) Insert the pillow form.

▲ 3. **Press the seam open and lay the** zipper face down along it. Sew in place from the right side. Undo the basting and open the zipper. Using your paper shape for the zig-zag trim, cut out four pieces of fabric.

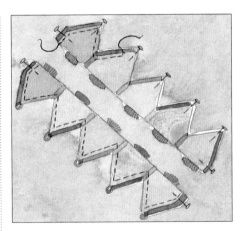

▲ 4. **Lay a tassel on each point of the** zig-zags on two of these pieces of fabric. Lay another piece of fabric on top to cover the tassels, and sew all around zig-zags. Carefully clip the corners and turn through to the right side, gently pulling the tassels at the points. Press.

# CLASSICAL

*Shiny artificial fibers, rich silks and simple muslins are*

*perfect for conjuring up ancient Greek columns and*

*decorative capitals. Combine graphite gray with off-whites*

*and add a few well-placed touches of gold.*

# golden drapes

*These curtains have a heavy, full appearance with the added luxury of a lining. They are attached to the pole by means of a heading tape. The dramatic effect is heightened by the twisted rope and gold cord tie-back.*

MATERIALS
◆ Fabric
◆ Lining
◆ Interfacing
◆ Heading tape and hooks
◆ Rope and tassels
◆ Gold cord or braid

CURTAIN – MEASURING UP
The width of each curtain is the length of the pole plus half again. The length is from pole to floor, plus extra length to break on the floor and another 4in (10cm) for the top and bottom hems. The measurements for the lining are the same, less 2in (5cm) on the width and 3in (7.5cm) on the length. You will need a strip of iron-on interfacing measuring the width of the curtain by 2in (5cm).

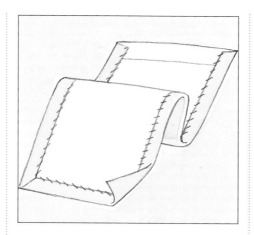

▲ I. **Press the iron-on interfacing onto** the wrong side of the fabric along the top edge. Turn the side and bottom hems of the main fabric over by 2in (5cm) and press. Miter the corners and stitch the hems in place.

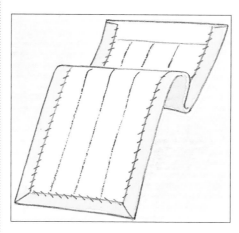

▲ 2. **Draw vertical lines down the** length of the fabric at distances of about 12in (30cm), using tailor's chalk and starting at the center.

3. **On the lining, turn under ⅝in** (1.5cm) along each side edge and at the bottom hem. Press. Miter the corners and stitch the hems in place. Lay the lining on the curtain, wrong sides together. It should sit 2in (5cm) from the top of the main fabric.

4. **Pin the lining to the main fabric** down the center, then fold back the lining so that the fold lies flat along the drawn center line. Sew the lining to the main fabric wth loose stitches.

▲ 5 **Stitch the lining to the main** fabric along each drawn line in this manner, working outward from the center. Smooth the lining to the sides and slip-stitch to the side and bottom hems.

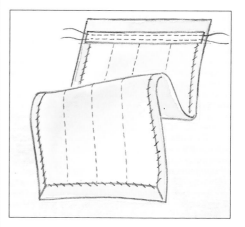

▲ 6. **Turn the top edge of the main** fabric over to the lining and cover the raw edge with heading tape. Turn under the tape ends and knot the cords. Stitch along all the edges of the tape, leaving the cords free. Gather up the cords as required and attach the hooks.

## TIE-BACK – MEASURING UP

Loop a tape measure loosely around the curtain at the desired height, holding the ends together against the wall. This will give you the tie-back length. If using a rope, add enough for the ends to hang down if required.

**1. If using a rope tie-back, cut the rope** and the gold cord to the required length. Wrap the gold cord neatly around the rope and stitch the ends in place to secure. Attach tassels to each end.

**2. Alternatively, cut two strips of fabric** to the required length and width, adding ⅝in (1.5cm) all around for seam allowances. Sew around three sides, turn right side out and slip-stitch the opening closed. Stitch gold braid around all four sides and sew a brass ring at each end to hook the tie-back to the wall.

**3. Allow the fabric of the drapes to** balloon slightly over the tie-back. Arrange the folds so that the lower hem of the curtain spreads attractively over the floor. Do not be too neat and fussy as a spontaneous look is best.

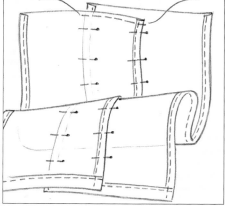

# sheer curtains

*These sheer or semi-sheer curtains are designed not to be pulled but to provide privacy and to allow diffused light to enter a room. They work well as under-curtains but also look stylish in their own right.*

## MATERIALS

◆ Lightweight fabric such as muslin

◆ 1½in (4cm) wide casing strip

◆ Plastic-covered curtain wire or thin brass rod

◆ Rope

## MEASURING UP

You will need two pieces of fabric, each one the same as the width of the window. Add 10in (26cm) to the required length for the top and bottom hems.

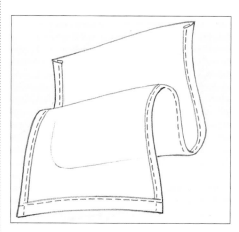

▲ **1. Turn in the sides of each piece of** fabric by ⅝in (1.5cm) and press. Repeat and sew. Turn up the bottom by 2in (5cm) and press. Repeat and sew.

▲ **2. At the top, mark each piece of** fabric in the center with a pin. Lay one piece of fabric over the other, both right side up, so that the side edge of one lines up with the center of the other. Check that all four side edges are parallel. Hold the two overlapping side hems in place with spaced pins. Baste the two pieces together at the top where they overlap.

**3. Turn over the top hem by 2½in** (6.5cm). Press. Pin the casing strip over the raw edge. Turn in the ends to neaten. Sew along the top and bottom edges, leaving the ends open.

**4. Pull the plastic-covered wire or the** brass rod through the casing and secure in place over the window. Arrange the gathers of the curtains and loop back with simple rope tie-backs.

# bed corona

*This is a really easy way to transform your bed into something glamorous and romantic. Its success relies on generous use of fabric, combined with stylish trimmings.*

### MATERIALS

◆ Fabric
◆ Metal hanging hooks or brass clips
◆ Brass or metal wall hooks
◆ Cord and tassels if required

### MEASURING UP

Measure the length of the bed. Each curtain should be as wide as this measurement. Decide on the length required and add 6in (15cm) for the hems.

**1. Hem the sides by turning ⅝in** (1.5cm) to the wrong side. Press. Repeat and sew. Turn up the bottom hem by 1½in (4cm) and press. Repeat and sew. Turn over the top hem by 1½in (4cm) and press. Repeat and sew. Press again.

**2. Attach the curtain to the corona** using either brass clips with sprung "teeth" or metal hanging hooks which can be inserted straight into the back of the top hem of the curtains. If the corona is fairly simple, use ties to attach it as these will give extra detail.

**3. Decide where to position the wall** hooks, making sure they are level with each other. Wrap each curtain twice around the hooks and allow the drape to fall to the floor. Adjust as necessary. If you want extra decoration, tie a cord around each of the knots of fabric and sew a tassel at each end.

# doric valance

*This is a sophisticated and glamorous valance. It looks best teamed with curtains in the same fabric. It is not difficult to make, but a certain amount of confidence is required to make decisions regarding proportions and pattern-making.*

## MATERIALS

◆ Fabric

◆ Thick cardboard for stiffening the circles

◆ Batten

◆ Braid and tassels

## MEASURING UP

Measure the width of your window, plus any additional width required. The length is the deepest point of the valance. The diameter of the doric spirals should be the same as the measurement of the deepest point of the valance or smaller, as preferred.

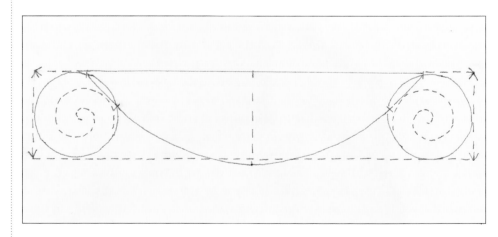

▲ **1. First, make a paper pattern. Cut a** rectangular paper shape based on the calculated dimensions. Fold it in half widthwise to find the center and tape it over the window. This gives you an idea, *in situ*, of the overall look. Draw two circles representing the outer spirals and a central curve for the drape, checking the scale and proportion in relation to the window. Use a dinner plate or round tray to help you draw the circles.

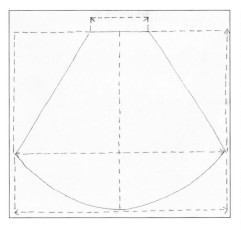

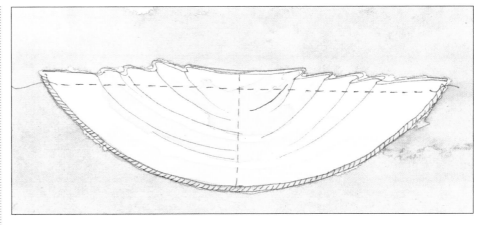

▲ **2. To make a pattern for the central** drape of fabric, cut a rectangle measuring 1½ times the finished width, by 2½ times the depth of the central drape. Add ⅝in (1.5cm) all around for seam allowances plus an extra 1½in (4cm) at the top for fixing to the batten. Draw and cut out the finished shape. For the rounded spirals, make two separate circular paper pieces. Add a 1in (2.5cm) seam allowance all around. Use this paper circle without seam allowances for the stiffener.

▲ **3. To make the central drape, cut** out two pieces of fabric. Lay them right sides facing one another and sew together ⅝in (1.5cm) in along the curved edge. Turn right side out and press. Sew braid along the curved edge. Pleat the top of the valance symmetrically until the width corresponds with the first paper shape showing the finished look. Sew the pleats into place securely.

**4. To make the circular shapes, cut two** circles of thick cardboard using the smaller circle of the paper pattern. Cut out two circles from the main fabric, incorporating the seam allowances. Cut out two more circles of main fabric to the same size as the stiffener. Put a small amount of glue around the edges of the cardboard circles. Carefully place the wrong side of the larger fabric circles onto the stiffener, smoothing down the fabric to prevent puckering.

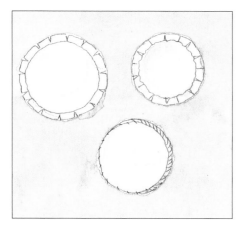

**◄ 5. Snip the seam allowances all** around. Press the allowance down carefully and evenly around the cardboard. Place the smaller fabric circles wrong-side down over the back of the stiffened circles and slip-stitch in place.

**► 6. Draw a spiral in chalk or pencil** on the right sides of the rounded shapes. Practice on the paper shapes first. Stitch braid around the drawn line, keeping it smooth and non-jerky.

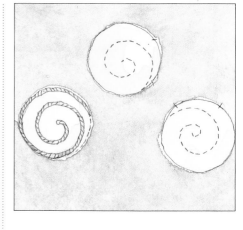

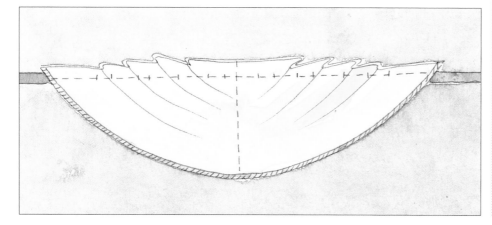

**◄ 7. Mark the center of the wooden** batten. Place the center of the drape in line with the center of the batten. Staple the drape to the batten at regular intervals, leaving 2in (5cm) of fabric unattached at either end. Do not worry if you make a mistake. Simply remove the staples and start again. The stapled edge will be hidden when the valance is mounted, so any small holes left in the fabric when staples are removed will not be visible.

**► 8. Thread a pair of tassels onto a** piece of string and use a needle to pull them through the center of each circle. Knot the string to secure. Twist the batten over so that the staples are at the back. Place the spiral circles at either end of the batten, with the top part of the curve overlapping the batten by ⅝in (1.5cm). Staple them securely in place from behind. Place the drape ends over the circular shapes and staple them to the batten. Check that all three pieces are secure and fix in place above the window.

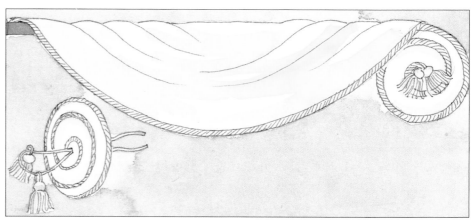

# triangle valance

*This sensational valance will give your room instant glamor. Make it with a length of fabric and some swooshy fringing or use an existing fringed square such as an antique shawl or a lacy tablecloth. All you need are some dramatic tassels and cords to fix it in place and the job's done.*

## MATERIALS

◆ Fabric

◆ Fringing

◆ Brass or wooden batten

◆ Cord and tassels

## MEASURING UP

This valance is based on a square which has been folded in half diagonally to form a double triangle. It must be sufficient to cover the width of the window plus some additional length to drape down on either side.

**1. Turn the edges of the square to the** right side by ⅜in (1cm) and press. Lay the fringe braid over the edge to conceal the raw edges. Sew the fringe in place, turning in the ends to neaten. Fold the square in half diagonally.

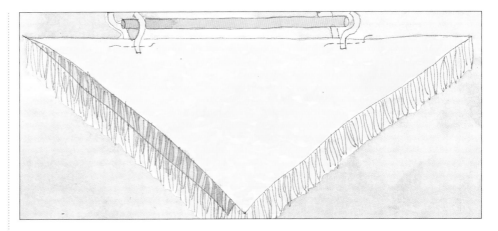

▲ **2. Mark the center of the folded** edge of the square. Measure half the batten length to either side of this mark, minus 2in (5cm). Sew tape or cord at these two points and tie to the batten. Fix the batten above the window.

**3. Loop cord around the fabric at each** end of the batten and tie in a firm knot. Wrap the cord around the batten a few more times, leaving enough to hang down either side of the window. Finish by sewing tassels to the ends.

# spiral bolster

*This is a simple but effective way of pulling seating areas into the look of the room by using pillows to echo the other soft furnishings.*

## MATERIALS

◆ Fabric
◆ Bolster form
◆ Iron-on interfacing
◆ Zipper
◆ Cord and tassels

## MEASURING UP

Cut a rectangle of fabric whose depth is the circumference of the bolster form plus 1½in (4cm) seam allowance. The length should be that of the bolster form plus 1¼in (2.5cm) for seams. The ends are two circles, whose diameter is that of the bolster plus ⅝in (1.5cm) all around for seams.

**1. Cut out two circles of fabric with a** seam allowance and two circles of interfacing without the allowance. Center the interfacing on the wrong side of the fabric circles. Iron them in place. Draw a generous spiral in chalk or pencil on the right side of the circles.

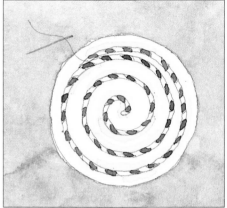

▲ **2. Pin cord along the drawn spiral** line. Sew the cord carefully and securely in place either by hand or machine.

**3. Fold the rectangle of fabric in half** lengthwise, right sides facing. Sew a 2in (5cm) long seam at each end. Baste the opening and press the seam open. Baste the zipper in place, wrong side up, along the basted seam. Turn the rectangle right side out, and sew the zipper in place from the right side. Undo the basting stitches and press. Open the zipper and turn wrong side out.

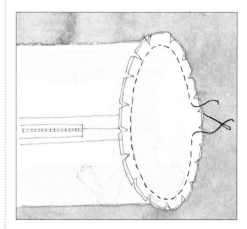

▲ **4. Place the circles at either end of** the main fabric, right sides facing one another. Pin all around the seams, leaving an allowance of ⅝in (1.5cm). Sew the seams and snip the allowance all around. Turn right side out and press. Put the bolster form into the cover and zip up the opening. Stitch a tassel at the center of each circle to finish.

# gathered bolster

*This is another simple but effective way of incorporating a sofa into the style of a room by using bolsters to echo curtains or valances.*

## MATERIALS

- ◆ Fabric
- ◆ Bolster form
- ◆ Iron-on interfacing
- ◆ Narrow cord
- ◆ Zipper
- ◆ Braid, buttons, and tassels

## MEASURING UP

Cut a rectangle of fabric whose depth is the circumference of the bolster form plus 1½in (4cm) seam allowance. The length should be that of the bolster form plus 1¼in (2.5cm) for seams. The gathered circular ends are made from rectangular strips of fabric whose width is the radius of the bolster end plus 1½in (4cm) either side for the seams. The length of each strip depends on the required amount of gathering, for example twice the circumference of the bolster plus 1¼in (3.5cm) for the seams.

**1. Take the two long strips of fabric for** the ends of the bolster. Turn ¼in (1cm) to the wrong side along one long edge of each. Press. Turn under again by ⅝in (1.5cm), press and sew. Make two buttonholes, 1in (2.5cm) apart at the center of the seams.

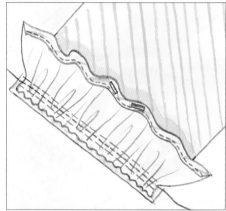

**▲ 2. Sew two parallel lines of gathering** stitches close together along the opposite long edge of each strip. The first row of gathering stitches should be ⅝in (1.5cm) in from the edge. Gather up to the width of the main fabric and tie off. Lay the gathered edge of each strip onto either end of the main fabric, right sides together. Sew a seam between the two rows of gathering.

**3. Open out the rectangle and press the** seam allowance toward the gathers. Fold in half lengthwise, right sides facing, and sew together with a ⅝in (1.5cm) seam. Press the allowance open.

**4. Turn the fabric tube right side out** and pull it over the bolster form. Thread a narrow cord through the buttonholes at each end and draw the fabric up until it closes over the form. Tie into a firm bow and push this inside the central hole to conceal. Sew a button and tassel over the center of the gathered ends.

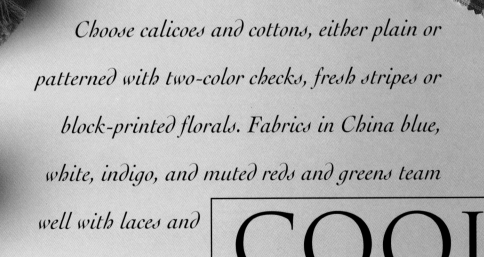

Choose calicoes and cottons, either plain or patterned with two-color checks, fresh stripes or block-printed florals. Fabrics in China blue, white, indigo, and muted reds and greens team well with laces and simple tassels.

# COOL CALICOES

# café curtain

*There are occasions when a window requires a treatment that will allow a certain amount of privacy, but where something more interesting than a traditional net curtain is necessary. This is a variation on the classic café curtain, and can be made in a variety of fabrics.*

## MATERIALS
◆ Fabric
◆ Grommets and grommet punch
◆ Cord
◆ Small tassels

MEASURING UP

Decide where the curtain will hang from – you might prefer to have a half-curtain, for example. Attach hooks from which to hang the curtain at this point. From this point down, measure the length. The width is the length of the pole plus half again. Allow 10in (25cm) for the top and bottom hems.

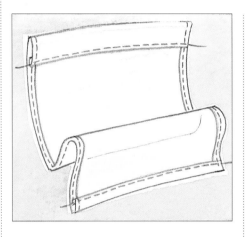

▲ **1. Hem the sides by turning over ⅝in** (1.5cm) to the wrong side. Press. Repeat, sew and press again. Turn the top and bottom hems by 2½in (6cm) and press. Repeat, sew and press again.

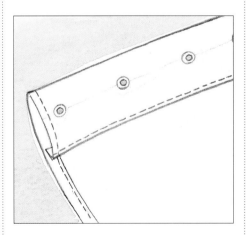

▲ **2. Mark a line across the center of** the top hem with chalk. Mark where the grommets are to be applied, making sure that they are evenly distributed.

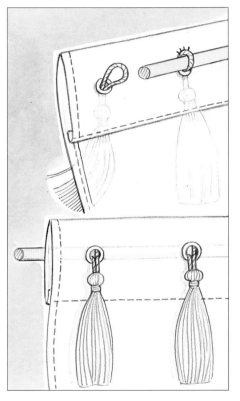

▲ **3. Cut the hanging cord to the** length desired. Thread a tassel through each of the grommets, from the front of the curtain so that the hanging loop of the tassel only is on the wrong side. Stitch the loop to the curtain, just above the grommet. Thread the cord through the tassel loops and hang in place.

# lacy curtain

*This curtain looks lovely with light filtering through the lace edging. Very easy to make, the impact depends on a good choice of border. Broderie anglaise would be an attractive alternative to lace.*

## MATERIALS

◆ Wide lace or broderie anglaise

◆ Cord and tassels

◆ Matching or contrasting fabric for the tie-back

## CURTAIN – MEASURING UP

Measure the length and width of the curtain. You will need this amount of edging lace plus approximately 5in (12.5cm) for the miter and turning in the ends to neaten.

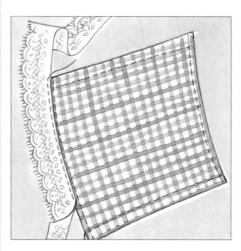

▲ **1. Lay the curtain flat, right side up.** Lay the lace edging on top of the side hem, also right side up, with the edge to be stitched overlapping the curtain slightly. Baste the lace in place, from the bottom hem up to the top hem. Stop at the corner.

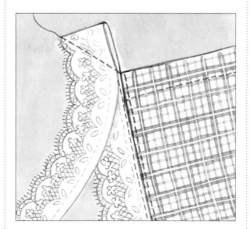

▲ **2. Fold the lace back on itself. Sew a 45° seam from the corner of the curtain to the outer edge of the lace. Trim away the fold to ¼in (6mm).**

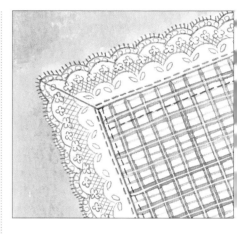

▲ **3. Continue basting the lace along** the top hem until you reach the other side. Machine-stitch the lace in place. Remove the basting stitches and press. Hang the curtain at the window.

## TIE-BACK – MEASURING UP

Loop your tape measure loosely around the curtain at the desired height and hold the ends together. This will be the finished length of the tie-back. Cut a fabric strip 1½ times this length by 3in (8cm) wide. Cut two pieces of lace trim to the same length as the fabric strip.

**1. Fold the fabric in half lengthwise.** Sew a seam ¼in (6mm) in from the edge. Turn right side out. Press. Turn in the ends and slip-stitch in place to neaten.

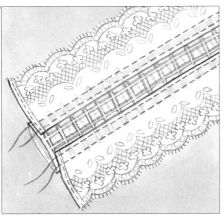

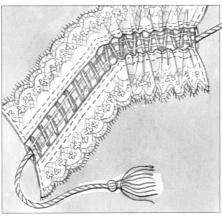

▲ **2. Lay a strip of lace along both** sides of the fabric tube so that they overlap the fabric by ⅝in (1.5cm). Sew along the edges of the lace and the fabric.

▲ **3. Thread the cord through the tube** of fabric and pull up to gather. Sew a tassel to each end of the cord. Tie the curtain back as desired.

# lace blind

*This is a basic blind which is lifted by the addition of a lace inset. A crisp linen or calico, or perhaps a ticking, are suitable fabrics. Look around for a shaped piece of lace or broderie anglaise; you might well find something in an antique shop specializing in textiles.*

## MATERIALS
◆ Crisp fabric
◆ Blind attachments
◆ Lace inset

## MEASURING UP

Cut a rectangle of fabric whose width is that of the pole, plus 2½in (5cm) for the hems. Add 4½in (11cm) to the length of the window for the hems.

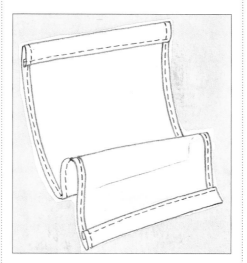

▲ **1. Hem the sides by turning ⅝in** (1.5cm) to the wrong side. Repeat and sew. Press crisply. Make the casings for the battens or poles by turning ⅝in (1.5cm) to the wrong side, top and bottom, and then a further 1½in (4cm). Sew along the folded edges.

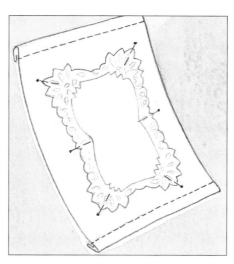

▲ **2. Pin the lace inset onto the right** side of the blind, positioning it as required. Tape the blind to the window to check the overall look. When you are satisfied, baste the lace in place.

▲ **3. Zig-zag stitch all around the lace** inset. Make sure that the stitches zig onto the lace and zag back onto the fabric. Remove the basting stitches.

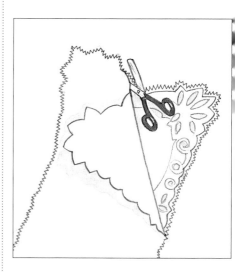

▲ **4. If using a sheer fabric, the light** should show through the lace. However, to emphasize this effect, cut away the fabric from behind the lace. Use round-ended scissors to avoid piercing the lace. Hang the blind in place.

# cottage curtain

*This lightweight curtain would look charming in an informal, cottage-type setting but could easily be translated into other styles by the use of different fabrics and trimmings. It is particularly suitable for small windows in darker rooms where you want to create a sense of privacy without blocking out the light. The cord-and-tassel "waist" is a simple but effective idea.*

## MATERIALS

◆ Lightweight fabric such as muslin, net or lace

◆ Lace trim for hems (optional)

◆ Plastic-covered curtain wire and hooks, or two poles

◆ Cord, ribbon or lace for "waist" tie

◆ Tassels

MEASURING UP

The length of the curtain is the same as that of the window frame, plus an allowance of 6in (16cm) for the hems. The width is the width of the window frame plus half again. You may prefer to use double for very thin fabrics. You will need sufficient curtain wire for two widths of the window frame.

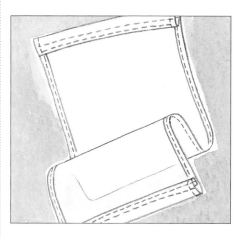

▲ **1. Hem the sides of the curtain by** turning over ⅝in (1.5cm) to the wrong side. Press. Repeat, sew and press again. Turn over the top and bottom hems by 1½in (4cm) each and press. Repeat and sew a line of stitching very close to the folded edge on both the top and bottom hems. Sew another line of stitching along both these hems, ⅝in (1.5cm) out from the first lines of stitching. These form the two channels for the curtain wires.

**2. The excess fabric on the outside of** the wire channels will gather together to form an attractive frill when the curtain is hung. Sew narrow lace or a similar trimming to the outer edge of the top and bottom hems if you want to exaggerate this feature even more.

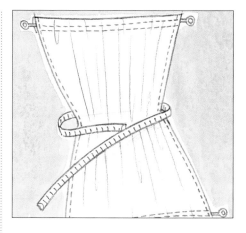

▲ **3. Thread the wire through the** channels and hook across the window. Loop a tape measure around the center of the curtain to decide on the length of cord required. Allow extra for tying and for the cord ends to hang down.

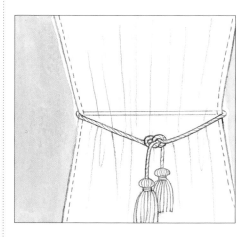

▲ **4. Sew a tassel to each end of the** cord and tie a "waist" around the curtain. Do not fasten the cord too tightly.

# padded headboard pillow

*A headboard pillow provides comfort, keeps out drafts, and enhances the decor of the bedroom. It might hang from a horizontal bar on, for example, a brass bed or simply lie against the wall. The pillow shown here is rectangular but it can echo other shapes in a room if preferred. A zipper at the back allows the padding to be removed easily for laundering.*

MATERIALS
◆ Fabric
◆ Batting
◆ Fringing
◆ Zipper
◆ Cord, braid or ribbon for ties (optional)

MEASURING UP

Cut two rectangles of fabric to the width of the bed and to the depth required. Add a ⅝in (1.5cm) seam allowance all around. If you prefer to make two separate pillows for a double-sized bed, alter the measurements accordingly. Add a further 1¼in (3cm) to the depth of the back piece for the zipper and cut the fabric into two pieces across its depth.

**1.** Lay the two back pieces of fabric on top of each other, right sides facing. Sew together along one long edge for 5in (12cm) at each end, leaving a gap in the center for the zipper. Baste the opening along the seam line and press.

**2.** Lay the zipper face down along the basted part of the seam. Baste the zipper in place. Turn the fabric over to the right side and machine-stitch the zipper in place. Remove the basting stitches and open the zipper.

**3.** Place the front and back together, right sides facing, and sew all around. If you wish to tie the pillow to a pole, position the ties between the two pieces of fabric and sew them firmly into the seam. Turn right side out and press.

**4.** Pin fringing all around the front of the pillow, positioning it so that it overlaps the edges and mitering the corners. Stitch in place, sewing through both pieces of fabric. Fill the pillow with wadding and close the zipper.

# fringed bolster

*This bolster is in calico but can be made in any number of fabrics, with different fringing and tassels, to suit the look you are trying to achieve. A bolster either end of a sofa is not only comfortable but provides a wonderful opportunity to show off interesting textures and trimmings.*

## MATERIALS
◆ Fabric
◆ Bolster form
◆ Fringing and rope cord
◆ Narrow cord and tassels

MEASURING UP

The width of the fabric should equal the circumference of the bolster form, plus 1¼in (3cm) for the seam allowance. The length needs to be that of the bolster form, plus the radius of each circular end and another 2in (5cm) for the casing.

1. Measure the length of the radius of the bolster form plus 1in (2.5cm) in from each end of the fabric. Draw a line with chalk at this point. Pin a length of fringing across each end so that the fringes butt up to the drawn lines. Pin another two lengths of fringing so that their straight edges butt up against those of the first two lengths. Sew in place along the straight edges and at the point where the tasseled fringe begins. Sew a length of rope cord across the center of both bands of fringing.

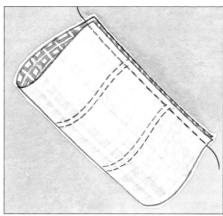

▲ 2. Fold the fabric in half lengthwise, right sides facing, and sew along this edge using a ⅝in (1.5cm) seam allowance. Press the seam open.

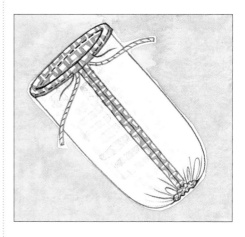

▲ 3. Turn in both ends of the bolster fabric by ¼in (6mm) and then ¾in (2cm) to make the casing for the gathering cord. Press and sew along the folded edges, leaving a gap at the center.
Thread a length of cord through the casing at each end. Turn the fabric right side out and insert the bolster form. Tie the gathering cords into tight bows. Sew a tassel to each end of the cords and push the bow inside the bolster.

# FRENCH

*French style is one of elegance and panache.*

*Choose tapestry weaves, trompe l'oeil*

*prints and damasks in muted colors —*

*rusts and ochers — with rich accents.*

*France is home to the guild of tassel-*

*making, so search for sumptuous*

*trimmings in glittering golds.*

# fabric-trimmed curtains

*The wide band around these curtains is mitered at the corners to produce a very neat trim. The same fabric is used to make the loops that attach the curtains to the pole. Instead of a coordinating print fabric, you could use a dramatic braid or contrasting ribbon. Here, extra fabric has been used to make a matching table cover.*

## MATERIALS
◆ Fabric for main curtain
◆ Fabric for outer band and loops

## MEASURING UP

For each curtain, cut the main fabric to the width of the pole, plus any additional fullness required. Cut each curtain to the length desired, less the width of the outer band. Cut strips of fabric for the outer band. The band should be long enough to go all around the outside edges of the curtain, so sew as many strips together as necessary. Here, the hanging loops have a finished width of 3in (7.5cm), so cut strips 7¼in (18cm) by 9in (23cm), including seam allowances.

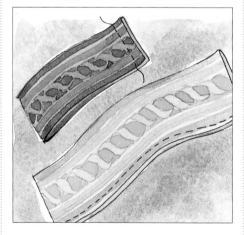

▲ **1. Make the loops by folding each** strip lengthwise, right sides together. Sew down the length, using a ⅝in (1.5cm) seam allowance. Turn right side out and press. Fold each strip in half widthwise and sew across the ends.

**2. Distribute the loops evenly along** the top edge of the curtain. Place them upside down on the wrong side of the fabric, raw edges even.

▲ **3. Starting at the bottom edge,** baste the outer band all around the outside edge of the main fabric. Both the main fabric and the contrasting strip should be wrong sides face up. Sew the band in place using a ⅝in (1.5cm) seam allowance all around.

▲ **4. Remove the basting stitches.** Next, miter the corners. Make a diagonal fold at each corner and sew a 45° seam. Trim the fold at the corners to ¼in (6mm) and press the seams open. Turn the band over to the right side of the fabric and press. Turn under the raw edge of the band by ⅝in (1.5cm) and press again. Starting at the bottom hem, top-stitch the inner edge of the band to the fabric.

▲ **6. Press the fabric band and hanging** loops crisply. This is a neat and formal style of trimming, so it is particularly important that all of the loops are the same length, so that the curtain will hang neatly and show the fabric trim to best effect.

**7. If you find that the loops are not** even, unpick the seam along the top edge of the curtain, reposition the appropriate loops and resew. Alternatively, make a small fold inward at the top edge of the appropriate loops and sew. Finally, slip the curtain pole through the loops and hang in place.

**8. Use a square of fabric to make a** matching table cover. Sew the outer band around all four sides, mitering the corners in the same way as for the curtains. If you have sufficient fabric, try making a multi-layered table cover. Simply make three separate covers, each one a little bigger than the others. Cover the table with the largest one first, with the smallest on top.

# rosette valance

*This valance is quick and easy to make. It has a double drape, although a single drape would work just as well. Its success relies on the generous cut of the fabric and a good choice of trimmings. This style will look perfect on its own or over light-weight under-curtains.*

## MATERIALS

◆ Fabric in two complementary colors
◆ Lining
◆ Cord
◆ Tassels

MEASURING UP

For the front part of the valance, measure the length of the pole and allow extra so that the fabric hangs down at the center. Add to this the desired length of fabric at the sides to give the overall length required. Experiment with the width to achieve the desired fullness – using a manufacturer's standard width is simplest and usually adequate. For the back twisted drape, experiment with a length of fabric, held in place by strong tape. This section of the valance reaches from end to end of the pole only.

**1. For the front part of the valance,** cut a piece of lining the same size as the main fabric. Put the two fabrics right sides together, aligning the edges. Sew around all four sides, leaving a gap of 4in (10cm) in the center of one side. Turn right side out and press. If using velvet, use a velvet board, putting the fabric right side down on the board. Slip-stitch the opening closed.

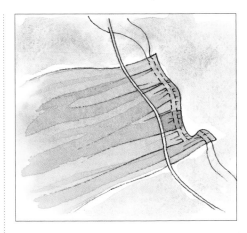

▲ **2. Line the back part of the valance** in the same way. If you are using a fabric that has no obvious right side, leave it as a single thickness. Run two rows of gathering stitches 1in (2.5cm) from each end. Pull the gathering up as tight as possible and wrap a length of cord around the ends to secure. Do not cut the ends of the cord.

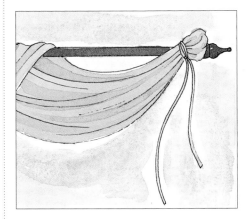

▲ **3. Twist the back valance piece** around the pole until the desired drape is achieved. Tie firmly in place at either end with the lengths of cord.

**4. For the front valance piece, mark the** center of the drape with a pin. Mark where the side drapes will begin (evenly on either side of the center pin) using more pins. Remove the central pin.

◀ 5. At the two remaining pin marks, fold the fabric back on itself and wrap a cord around the folds. Tie the cord tightly and arrange the gathered "knot" into a rosette effect. Leave the cord ends long. Tape or pin your fabric to the pole until the drape is right, and then wrap the cord ends around the pole to tie it firmly in position.

▶ 6. Decide on the finished length of the cords. Finish by sewing tassels to the ends to neaten and trim the cords.

# ottoman

*An ottoman is easy to transform whenever you want to change the style of a room. If you have a rather shabby specimen which could do with a change of upholstery, this is your chance to show off your sewing skills. It is important to make the finished product look as professional as possible. Therefore, do not be tempted to rush the job; be prepared to pin and re-pin, baste and re-baste. Your chosen trims should be taut and smooth in line and ends should not show.*

MATERIALS
◆ Fringing
◆ Rosettes
◆ Metal studs

MEASURING UP

Simply hold a tape measure in place around whatever part of the ottoman you wish to trim. Add a little extra to allow for neatening the edges.

▲ I. **Measure the depth of your** fringing and draw a line around the base of the ottoman this amount above the floor. Make sure that it is even all the way around, pinning the fringing in place first to check. Sew firmly in place, always checking that it is level.

▲ 2. **Sew fringing around the top** of the ottoman, just below the lid. Leave space for a row of metal studs, if required. A row of studs around the edges of the lid may also look good. Sew a rosette and pair of tassels to each corner of the lid of the ottoman.

# table cover

This table cover is designed simply for decorative use. It can be used as a foil for a display of china or a bowl of flowers, or to make a table which is used only occasionally look sophisticated and interesting. Make it double-sided, in contrasting fabrics and colors, so that it is reversible. A table cover is the perfect subject for a speedy trimmings treatment.

## MATERIALS

◆ Reversible fabric or two contrasting colors of fabric

◆ Fringing

◆ Cord and tassels

## MEASURING UP

Measure the table top and consider how far you want the fabric to hang down over the sides. Add a ⅝in (1.5cm) seam allowance all around.

**1. If making your own reversible** fabric, lay the two pieces together, right sides facing one another. Sew all around the four sides, leaving a gap of 6in (15cm). Turn the fabric right side out and press. Slip-stitch the gap closed.

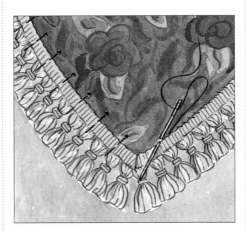

▲ **2. Pin and then baste the edge of the** fringing to the edge of the cloth. Leave a small overlap at the end and turn it under to neaten. Miter the corners.

▲ **3. Cut a short length of cord for** each corner of the table cover. Sew a tassel to both ends of each piece of cord. Make a small bow with each one and sew the center of the bows to the corners of the table cover.

# dramatic drapes

*A soft fabric which hangs well
would be ideal for this classic
French look, which makes a stylish
frame for an arch or window or,
as in this case, coordinates with
bedwear. These drapes are made
in three separate sections, all of
which are lined.*

MATERIALS

◆ Fabric

◆ Lining

◆ Cord

◆ Batten

◆ Fringing and tassels

MEASURING UP

You will need a long batten for the
central drape and two short battens for
the side swags. Loop a piece of string
from one end of the long batten to the
other. Tie it to the center of the batten
with a second length of string. Adjust
the two pieces of string to achieve an
attractive drape. For the two side swags,
measure the longest and shortest points
where you want the material to hang.

▲ **I. Start by making a paper pattern**
for half the drape. For the width,
measure the long batten from one end to
the center. For the depth, multiply the
length of the central piece of string by
2½. Draw out this rectangular shape and
then add a shallow curve at the bottom
edge. Cut out the paper shape and tape it
to the batten to check the look and
dimensions. Adjust as necessary.

**2. Place the paper shape onto a large**
piece of folded paper so that one long
edge of the paper shape aligns with the
fold. Draw around the shape and then
open out the folded piece of paper. Cut
out this new shape, adding ⅝in (1.5cm)
all around for seam allowances. This
forms the pattern for the whole drape.

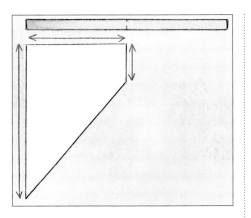

▲ **3. For the side swags, cut a rectangle** of paper to the width of half the batten and to the length of the longest point where you want the swag to reach. Measure down one edge where the shortest point of the swag will be and cut a diagonal line from here to the lowest corner. Pleat the paper shape and tape it to the end of the batten to check the overall look. Adjust as necessary. When cutting out the fabric, add seam allowances of 2in (5cm) to the edges which will be joined to the batten, and ⅝in (1.5cm) around all the other edges.

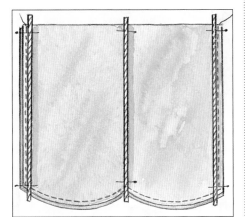

▲ **4. Cut one piece of fabric and one of** lining for the drape. Put the two pieces together, right sides facing. Cut three lengths of cord and pin them to the sides and center of the drape. Sew all along the curved edge and up the sides of the drape, making sure that the ends of the cords are firmly sewn into this seam.

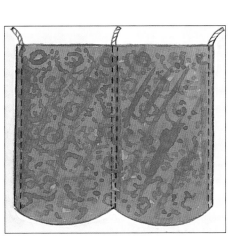

▲ **5. Turn the fabric through to the** right side and press. Adjust the three cords between the two layers so that the two outer ones lie parallel to the sides and the center one lies vertically down the center of the drape. Pin the cords in place. Sew down the inner edges of the two outer cords, and down both sides of the center cord.

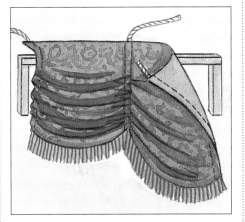

▲ **6. Apply the fringing to the curved** edges of the drape, leaving the cords hanging free. Tape the top edge of the drape to the batten, centers aligned. Pull up the three cords to the desired position and tie off. Staple the top edge of the drape to the batten and staple the sides to the side battens.

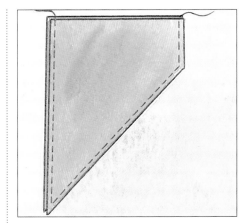

▲ **7. For the side swags, cut a pair of** fabric pieces and a pair in lining. Match the fabric pieces to the lining pieces, right sides facing and edges aligned. Sew down the longest side, along the diagonal line and up the shortest side.

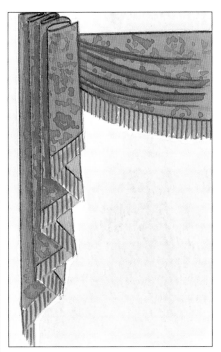

▲ **8. Turn right side out and press.** Apply the fringing to the diagonal hem. Pleat the top edge, fold it over the top of the batten, and staple in place so that the swags cover the sides of the drape. Finish by sewing a tassel at the longest point of both side swags and a pair of tassels at the center point of the drape.

# easy trimmings for pillows

*Here are a variety of ideas for trimming a basic square pillow. Buy or make a simple pillow in an appropriate fabric and enhance the look with carefully chosen trimmings. You will find that even with the minimum of skills you can produce results that will be exciting and stunning.*

## MATERIALS

◆ Pillows

◆ Braids, cords and fringing

◆ Rosettes, ribbons and tassels

MEASURING UP

Measure the circumference of the pillow to find the length of trimming necessary.

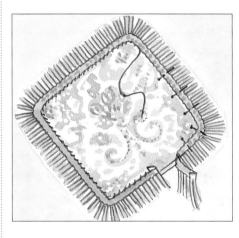

▲ **1. To attach fringing, pin the** braided edge around the edges of the pillow, close to the seams. Overlap the two cut ends of the trimming, turning them under to neaten. Slip-stitch firmly in place all around the edge nearest the seams of the pillow. Remove the pins and then slip-stitch the other edge of the braid to the pillow fabric.

▲ **2. An even simpler pillow treatment** can be achieved by attaching rosettes and tassels to each corner. First, pin them in place and then handsew firmly into position. Use toning thread.

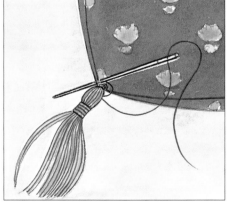

▲ **3. If you cannot find a tassel with a** rosette attached, a standard tassel will do just as well. Sew it to the corner of the pillow by hand. Loop the thread around the corner several times to strengthen the stitching in the same way as you would when sewing on buttons.

## ALTERNATIVE IDEAS

When you are making some of the other projects in this book, always save the left-over scraps of trimmings. You can use these to decorate small items such as pillows. However, if you do not have enough., you can use lots of other decorative braids or make your own from contrasting pieces of fabric or cords.

▲ I. If using strips of fabric as trimming, press the edges to the wrong side first to prevent fraying. Sew tassels to the corners.

◀ 2. Cut a length of braid and sew a line of gathering stitches along one edge. Pull up until a rosette is formed. Stitch a button on top and attach tassels to make your own rosette. Twist two cords together and sew this around the side seams of the pillow.

▶ 3. Instead of tassels, use ribbon. Make a decorative bow and sew a button in the center. The bow can have several loops rather than just two.

# FABULOUS FLORA

*Landscaped gardens, fields of wild flowers, swags*

*and bouquets – flowers are an enormous source*

*of inspiration and the choice of fabrics and*

*trimmings is myriad, with colors*

*ranging from pastels*

*to strong hues.*

# appliqué curtain

*This curtain has an appliqué flower-print detail which can be used to coordinate the curtain with other furnishings in the room. Look for a print which offers a defined outline that can be followed to create the shape of the heading. With the help of press-on interfacing, these curtains are much easier to make than they look.*

## MATERIALS

◆ Print fabric

◆ Sheer fabric, e.g. polyester, muslin

◆ Double-sided iron-on interfacing

MEASURING UP

For the sheer fabric, the width of the curtain should be the length of the pole plus any additional fullness required. The length should be as desired plus 4in (10cm) for the heading and the hem. For the print fabric, you will need sufficient to make the heading detail. This is the width of the curtain by the maximum depth suggested by the print. You will need extra print fabric for the ties. Use either sheer or print fabric for the facing, and cut it to the width of the curtain by 2in (5cm) deep. The interfacing should be the same size as the appliqué print heading.

▲ **I. Cut a strip of print fabric the** width of the curtain by the maximum depth. Cut the same shape in interfacing, Peel the backing off one side of the interfacing and lay it on the wrong side of the print. Press with an iron until the two layers are fused. On the right side of the print, draw a line with chalk using the print design as a guideline. With a sharp pair of scissors or a craft knife, cut along the line from one side to the other.

**2. Peel the backing off the other side** of the interfacing and lay the fused strip onto the right side of the sheer fabric, top straight edges aligned. Press until fused. Zig-zag stitch around the cut chalk line to secure the fabric edge.

**3. Next, hem the sides. Turn ⅝in** (1.5cm) to the wrong side and press. Repeat, sew and press again. Turn up the bottom hem by 1.5in (4cm) and press. Repeat, sew and press again.

▲ **4. Make the ties by cutting as many** strips as required. Each strip should measure 2in (5cm) wide by 9in (22cm) long. Fold each strip lengthwise, with the sides into the center. Open out and fold up one of the ends. Press. Refold the strip and sew along the long edge and across the folded end. Press. Lay the strips in pairs along the top of the curtain, on the right side, with raw edges aligned with the top of the curtain.

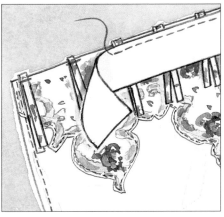

▲ **5. With the curtain the right side** up, lay the strip of facing across the top edge, with the ends pressed in. Sew through all the layers from one side to the other, making sure that the ties are firmly caught into the seam.

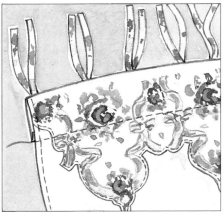

▲ **6. Turn the facing over to the wrong** side. Turn up the long raw edge of the facing a little and press. Sew around all three edges. Press the facing and the ties. Tie the curtain to the pole and adjust the fullness as desired.

# frilly curtains

*Choose a summery print to make a pretty frame for a cottage-style window. The sides are edged with braid and a tassel sewn at the top and echoed in the tasseled tie-back. The heading forms a pretty frill.*

## MATERIALS

- ◆ Fabric
- ◆ Iron-on interfacing
- ◆ Heading tape and hooks
- ◆ Braid and tassels

## MEASURING UP

The width of each curtain is the length of the pole plus any additional fullness required. The length will be as desired plus 10in (25cm) for the heading and the bottom hem.

**1. First, hem the sides of the curtains.** Turn ⅝in (1.5cm) to the wrong side and press. Repeat, then sew and press again. Turn up the hem by 1.5in (4cm). Repeat, sew and press again. Cut two strips of interfacing, one for each curtain, measuring the finished width by 2in (5cm) in depth. Press each strip onto the wrong side of the top of each curtain, 3½in (9cm) down from the top edge. Turn the top 3½in (9cm) of the fabric to the wrong side and press.

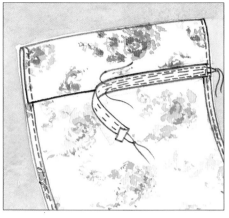

▲ **2. Cover the remaining raw edge of** fabric with heading tape. Position the tape so that 3in (7.5cm) of fabric at the top of the curtain is left free to form the frill. Turn under the tape ends, tie off the cords, and sew around all four sides of the tape, leaving the cords free.

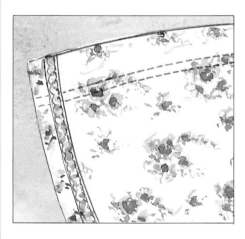

▲ **3. Sew braid down the inside edge of** each curtain, approximately 2in (5cm) in from the edge. Remember to turn in the ends to neaten.

**4. Pull up the gathering cords on the** heading tape to the desired width and finish by knotting. Attach the hooks to the tape and hang the curtains. The top edge of the fabric will fall forward to create a pretty frill.

# celebration setting

*Special occasions deserve a special table setting. Your guests' reactions will make you glad you spent a little time and effort creating this wonderful celebration setting.*

## MATERIALS

◆ Fabric

◆ Festoon curtain tape

◆ Fringing, cord and tassels

## MEASURING UP

Divide the table into four equal quadrants. Tape a piece of string to the outer edges of the table and allow it to hang between two adjacent quadrant marks. Use this to decide the depth of the required "drape." Double the measurement from the edge of the table to the depth of the drape. Add this to the measurement from the center of the table to the edge, and this is the circumference of the circle that you will need to cut.

**1. Cut a paper circle to the required** circumference. You may need to join several pieces of paper together. With a pencil, draw the quarter sections on the circle and the circumference of the table top onto the paper, centrally positioned.

**2. Cut out the circle of fabric. You may** need to join several widths of fabric together first if the table is quite large. Transfer the table top circumference and the four quarter sections to the wrong side of the fabric using a piece of chalk.

▲ **3. Cut four lengths of festoon tape** and pin one down each of the chalked quarter lines on the wrong side of the fabric, from the table top edge to the edge of the fabric. Stitch in place. Turn up a ½in (1cm) hem all around the circle and press. Turn up by the same amount again and press. Pin the fringing to the right side of the fabric and sew in place.

**4. Cover the table with the circle and** pull up the cords in the festoon tape to create the desired drape. Tie the cords to hold the drape in place and sew tassels onto the ends to finish.

# appliqué blind

*This blind works well when a window needs to be permanently covered but where a more attractive treatment than a basic blind is required. Choose a floral fabric with individual motifs that can easily be cut out. Here, the motifs are arranged along the bottom edge of the blind, a large central motif and two smaller ones at the corners, but you might want to cover the whole blind in motifs. The appliqué method is easy to do, but cutting out the fabric shapes can be time-consuming.*

## MATERIALS

◆ Lightweight sheer fabric
◆ Floral fabric
◆ Double-sided iron-on interfacing
◆ Batten

### MEASURING UP

The blind width is the length of the batten plus 1in (2.5cm) for seams. The length should be that of the window plus 4in (10cm) for hems. You will need sufficient interfacing to cover the back of each of the flower motifs. Cut strips of floral fabric for ties, each measuring 6in (15cm) by 1½in (4cm).

**1. Hem the sides of the blind by** turning ¼in (6mm) to the wrong side. Press. Repeat, sew and press again. Turn over the top and bottom hems to the wrong side by 1in (2.5cm) and press. Repeat, sew and press again.

▲ **2. Press the floral fabric. Cut roughly** around the pieces to be appliquéed. Cut out similar shapes in the interfacing. Lay the interfacing onto the wrong side of the floral motifs and press in place. When they have bonded, cut carefully around the edges of the motifs. It is important to do this part thoroughly, working close to the edges of the motifs. Lay the motifs onto the right side of the blind fabric and check their position.

▲ **3. When you are satisfied, mark the** position with pins. Peel off the backing on the other side of the interfacing and lay the motifs onto the blind fabric, using the pins as guides for position. Press until bonded.

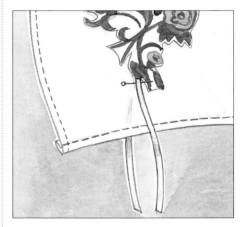

▲ **4. Make the ties by turning up the** ends of each one by ½in (1.5cm) to the wrong side. Press the long sides into the center on the wrong side. Put the folded edges together and sew down the length and across the ends. Sew the ties to the base of the lower corner appliqué motifs, one at the front and one at the back. Loosely roll up the bottom corners of the blind and fasten the ties into a bow. Staple the top edge of the blind to the batten and hang in place.

# rosette swag

*This rosette swag adds further decorative detail to a curtain-and-valance window treatment. It looks best when made either in the same or a coordinating fabric, but use a strongly colored contrasting fabric for the lining to emphasize the detail of the swag.*

## MATERIALS

◆ Fabric

◆ Lining

◆ Self-covering button

## MEASURING UP

Measure the longest point where you want the side swag to reach. Measure half the width of the window. Draw a rectangle to these measurements and mark the depth of the central drape of the valance onto the edge of the rectangle opposite the longest point of the swag. Draw a diagonal line between these two points. Add ⅝in (1.5cm) all around for seam allowances. Decide on the diameter of the rosette and cut a strip of fabric to this width by 14in (35cm) long, plus ⅝in (1.5cm) for seam allowances.

**1. First, make a paper pattern. Cut out** the paper shape following the guidelines for measuring up. Pleat the paper shape and tape it in place to check the overall look. Adjust as necessary.

**2. Cut a pair of fabric pieces and a pair** in lining. Remember to reverse the pattern to get symmetrical swags for each end of the valance. Match the fabric pieces to the lining pieces, right sides facing and edges aligned. Sew around all four sides, leaving an 8in (20cm) gap along the top edge.

**3. Turn right side out and press. Slip-**stitch the opening closed. Pleat the top edge and pin the swag in place to check the look. Adjust as necessary and then staple or sew firmly in place. (The rosette will cover the stitching or staples.)

**▲ 4. Fold the strip of fabric for the** rosette in half widthwise, right sides facing. Sew across the ends. Fold it in half along its length, wrong sides together, and press. Sew two rows of gathering stitches along the raw edges and pull up tightly. Stitch in place at the top pleat of the swag. Cover a button with matching fabric and sew to the center of the rosette.

# pleated lampshade

*A lampshade is very easy to make. You can either use a basic wire frame, buy an inexpensive lampshade to redecorate, or re-cover an existing lampshade that no longer suits your tastes.*

## MATERIALS
◆ Fabric
◆ Fringing

### MEASURING UP

Measure the circumference of the lampshade at its largest point and add half again. Measure the depth of the shade and add 3in (7.5cm) for hems. Cut a rectangle of fabric to this size.

**1. Turn ⅝in (1.5cm) of fabric over to** the wrong side along each long edge of the rectangle and sew. Turn ⅝in (1.5cm) to the wrong side along each shorter edge and press. Repeat, sew and press again. Pin one of the shorter edges to the existing lampshade or frame so that 1in (2.5cm) of fabric overlaps the top and bottom edges.

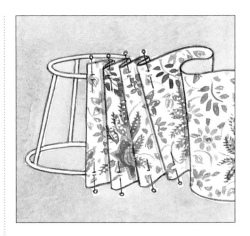

▲ **2. Pleat the top of the fabric, using** pins to hold the pleats in place. Adjust as necessary until the fabric is evenly pleated all around and fits snugly around the base frame.

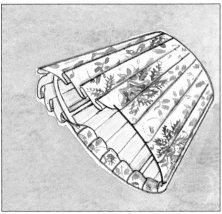

▲ **3. Turn the top pleated edge over to** the inside of the lampshade by 1in (2.5cm). Stitch in place. Pleat the bottom edge of the fabric in the same way, again turning it to the inside of the lampshade and securing in place.

**4. Sew a length of fringing around the** lower edge of the lampshade. Make sure that the fringing hangs down evenly all around the lampshade.

# mix-and-match ideas

*Soft furnishings are the ideal way to revitalize your furniture. A basic chair can be brought into the look of the room with this simple pillow and a few lengths of fringing. It does not matter if you do not have enough of one particular fringing to fit around both the pillow and the chair, simply try to match the dominating colors.*

MATERIALS
◆ Fabric
◆ Pillow form
◆ Braid
◆ Fringing

MEASURING UP
For the front of the pillow, measure the width and depth of the pillow form and add ⅝in (1.5cm) all around for seam allowances. For the back piece, add 5in (13cm) to the depth and cut in half across the depth.

**I. Join the two back pieces together in** the same way as the Picture-frame Pillow on the facing page.

▲ **2. Lay a length of fringing around** all four sides of the front piece. The fringing should be on the right side of the fabric with the straight edge even with the raw edges of the fabric. Baste in place. Lay the back square right side down on top. Sew around all four sides and then turn right side out.

▲ **3. Pin matching braid around the** chair. It should be positioned at the very edge of the fabric and cover as many edges as possible except for the lower ones. Sew fringing around these, making sure that it hangs down evenly.

# picture-frame pillow

*This decorative pillow features a floral motif as the centerpiece. The crossed-corner border forms an attractive "picture frame."*

## MATERIALS

◆ Fabric

◆ Pillow form

◆ Braid

◆ Tassels

MEASURING UP

You will need a front piece of fabric whose width and depth are those of the pillow form, plus 6in (15cm) for the self-edge border and seam allowances. For the back piece, add 5in (13cm) to the depth and then cut in half across the depth of the fabric.

**1. Take the two halves of the back** piece and turn ⅝in (1.5cm) to the wrong side along the cut edge of each. Press. Turn the same amount again, sew and press. Overlap the hemmed edges by 2in (5cm). Baste together across the ends.

▲ **2. On the front piece, draw two** parallel lines with chalk on the right side of the fabric, 3in (7.5cm) from the edge. Lay a strip of braid along each chalk line and baste in place. Repeat for the other two edges.

▲ **3. Place a tassel at each corner,** slipping the ends under the basting stitches. Sew around all the edges of the braid, securing the tassels as you do so.

**4. Lay the front and back pieces** together, right sides facing, and sew all around using a ⅝in (1.5cm) seam allowance. Turn through to the right side and press. Sew a line of stitching along the braid edge to define the pillow form. Press and insert the form.

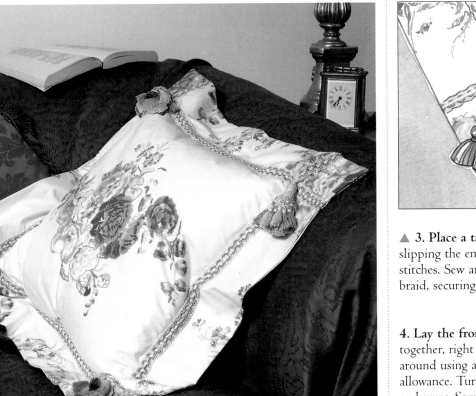

# RUSTIC

*Rough, unprocessed fabrics such as linen and muslin in beiges, ecrus and off-whites echo the simplicity of wood, flagstones and rush matting. Choose toning trimmings or treat with "vegetable" dyes to add a smattering of color.*

# linen and loops

*The loops on this curtain make a stylish change from more conventional hanging techniques. Use narrow loops to allow the curtain to be opened wide; wider loops work well for a dress curtain. Linen often comes in narrow widths and so you may need to join several lengths together. Sometimes it comes with an attractive red selvage which can be seamed to give the appearance of stripes. The heavy rope tie-back with large linen tassels complete the look.*

## MATERIALS

◆ Linen

◆ Wide fabric braid (optional)

◆ Heavy rope tie-backs with tassels

MEASURING UP

Each curtain should be the width of the pole, plus any additional fullness required. Add 5in (12.5cm) to the length for the hems. For linen loops with a finished width of 3in (7.5cm), cut strips 7in (18cm) by 9in (23cm), including allowances. The facing fabric should be with width of the curtain, plus 3in (7.5cm), by 4in (10cm) in depth. Alternatively, use wide braid for the loops and facing.

**1. First, hem the sides of the curtains.** Turn over ⅝in (1.5cm) to the wrong side and press. Repeat, then sew and press again. Turn up the bottom hem by 2in (5cm) and press. Repeat, sew and press again.

▲ **2. If making fabric loops, fold each** strip in half lengthwise, right sides together. Sew down the length ½in (1cm) in from the edge. Turn through to the right side and press. Fold over widthwise to form a loop and sew across the raw edge. Repeat for as many loops as required.

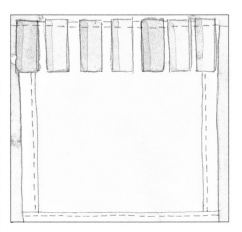

▲ **3. Baste the loops along the top of** the curtain. To make a feature of the facing, place them on the wrong side of the fabric; otherwise, on the right side.

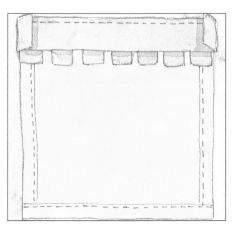

▲ **4. Lay the facing across the loops,** right side face down. Sew through the facing, loops and curtain, using a 1in (2.5cm) seam allowance. Turn in the ends to neaten and turn up the hem by 1in (2.5cm). Turn the facing over to the other side of the in main fabric and sew.

**5. To give the loops extra durability,** make the two outer ones slightly longer than the others and sew them in place so that there is a loop end on either side of the main fabric. Alternate loops could be attached in this way for decorative effect.

# tie-on curtain

*This lightweight curtain looks good with narrow, flat ties which attach it to the curtain pole. It can be used as an under-curtain for the heavier linen curtain on page 74, or on its own, providing privacy without blocking out the light.*

## MATERIALS

◆ Muslin or similar fabric

### MEASURING UP

For the main curtain, use the guidelines for the linen curtain on page 74. For the fabric ties, cut as many strips as required, each 2in (5cm) wide by 10in (26cm) long. For the facing, cut a strip of fabric as wide as the curtain, plus an allowance to turn in at the sides, by a depth of 3in (8cm).

**1. For the main curtain, hem the sides** and bottom as instructed for the linen curtains on page 74.

**2. To make the ties, fold in both long** sides of each strip toward the center, wrong sides together, and press. Open out again and then fold in ⅝in (1.5cm) at one of the shorter ends. Press again.

▲ **3. Refold the long sides of the strip** and then fold it lengthwise again so that the folded edges meet and the raw edges are enclosed. Press. Sew down the length of the strip and across the turned-under end. Repeat for all the ties.

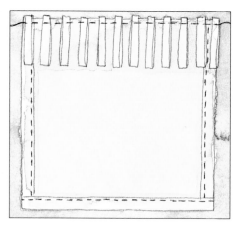

▲ **4. Lay pairs of ties, one on top of** the other, along the upper edge of the curtain on the wrong side and with raw edges even. Baste in place.

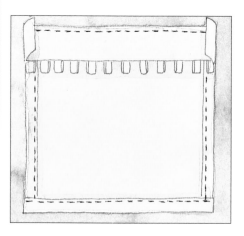

▲ **5. Lay the facing right side down** across the top of the curtain. Sew through the facing, ties, and curtain, ⅝in (1.5cm) in from the edge.

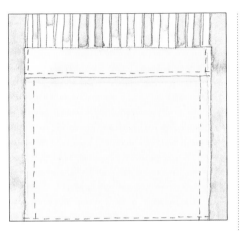

▲ **6. Turn the facing over to the right**
side, and then turn in the sides and lower
edge by ⅝in (1.5cm) to neaten. Press.
Top-stitch along the pressed edges. Press
the curtain and the ties to look crisp. Tie
the ties in knots or bows and thread the
pole through. Hang in place.

**7. To use these curtains on a corona or**
four-poster bed, measure the
circumference of the bed and treble this
to produce generous swathes of fabric.
Attach the ties as already described. Tie
the curtain directly onto the corona or
onto brass rings first.

**8. If you want to make a matching tie-**
back, make three more fabric ties. Each
one should be twice the required finished
length of the tie-back. Knot the three ties
together at one end. Braid them together
loosely and knot the other end when
finished. Anchor the knots over a brass
hook on the wall.

# fringed blind

*This attractive blind gives a decorative boost to any window. It is easy to make and provides diffused light and privacy whether rolled up or pulled down.*

## MATERIALS

◆ Muslin or similar fabric

◆ 2 wooden battens or ready-made blind fixings

◆ Fringing

◆ Tassel and cord

## MEASURING UP

Cut a rectangle of fabric to the width of the window, plus 2½in (6cm) for the hems. For the length, measure the depth of the window and add 3¼in (8cm) for the hems. The casing for the lower batten should be the width measurement, plus 1¼in (3cm), by the depth of the batten, plus 1¼in (3cm).

**1. Hem the sides. Turn ⅝in (1.5cm) to** the wrong side and press. Repeat, sew and press again. Do the same for the bottom hem. Decide where the lower batten is to be positioned (here, it is a third of the way up from the bottom of the window). Lightly draw a line from one side to the other, using either a hard pencil or tailor's chalk and checking that the line is exactly at right angles to the sides.

**2. Turn in the long edges of the casing** strip by ⅝in (1.5cm) and press. Turn in the ends by ⅝in (1.5cm), press and sew. Lay the strip across the width of the blind on the wrong side, using the drawn line as a guide. Sew along the top and bottom edges only. Press.

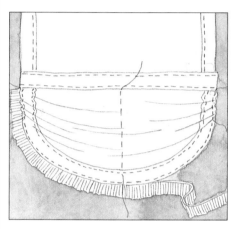

▲ **3. Sew the fringe to the hem, turning** in the ends to neaten. Mark the center of the hem with a pin. Next, gather up the sides of the blind from hem to casing, using small gathering stitches. Finish the gathering stitch securely. Run a gathering stitch from the pin on the center hem straight up to the casing.

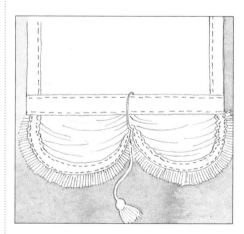

▲ **4. Slot in the lower batten. Gather** up the center and secure by sewing a piece of cord around the batten. Knot securely and leave a length of cord hanging. Fold the top hem of the blind over a batten by 2in (5cm) and staple in position. Fix the blind in the window and adjust to suit. Sew a tassel to the end of the hanging cord.

# tie-on chair covers

*This tie-on trim can be used for any piece of upholstery. Team it with tie-on curtains or a detail on a pillow. Not only is it decorative, it can be extremely useful in situations where soft covers do not quite fit the furniture. Either way, it is fun and easy to do.*

## MATERIALS

◆ Fabric to match or contrast
  with covers

MEASURING UP

Decide the length and width of the ties. Those shown measure 18in (46cm) in length by 1¼in (3cm), plus seam allowances of ⅝in (1.5cm) all around.

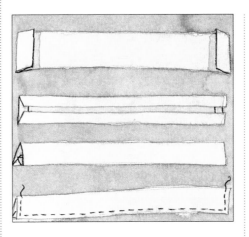

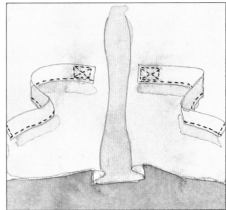

▲ **1. Fold in ⅝in (1.5cm) to the wrong** side along all four edges of each strip. Press. Fold in half lengthwise and press. Sew down the length of each strip and across the ends. Press.

▲ **2. Pin the pairs of strips to the cover** in the desired positions. Check the effect and adjust as necessary. Sew the strips firmly in place with a checked rectangle of stitches.

# linen pillow

*This is a very easy-to-make style of pillow with a self-bordered edge and easy-to-apply corner detail.*

## MATERIALS

◆ Linen

◆ Square pillow form

◆ Grommets and grommet punch

◆ Cord and tassels

## MEASURING UP

For the front piece of fabric, measure the pillow form and add 5¼in (13cm) to both the width and depth for the fabric border and seam allowances. For the back piece, add a further 4½in (11cm) to the depth, and cut in half across the depth.

▲ **I. First, make up the back of the** pillow. Turn under ⅝in (1.5cm) to the wrong side along one long edge of each half. Repeat and sew in place. Press both hems. Overlap the hemmed edges by 2in (5cm) and baste them together at each end.

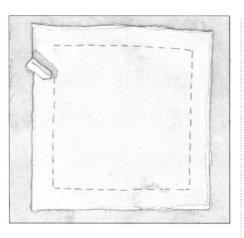

▲ **2. Lay the front piece on the joined** back pieces, right sides together, and sew around all four sides, using a ⅝in (1.5cm) seam allowance. Turn right side out and press. Draw a chalked line 2in (5cm) in from the edge around all four sides. Zig-zag stitch along this line and press. Insert the pillow form.

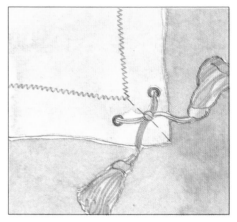

▲ **3. As a guide, draw a chalked line at** each corner, from the zig-zag stitching to the outer edge. Insert a grommet on either side of these lines. The grommets should be equidistant from the line and in the center of the self-edge border. Thread a cord through each pair of grommets and trim with tassels.

# tie-on chair pillow

*By providing freshness and color, a tie-on pillow can give a chair a new lease of life. It is also quicker to produce and less expensive than re-upholstering. A set of dining chairs given this treatment can make a tremendous impact.*

## MATERIALS
◆ Fabric
◆ Square pillow form
◆ Tassels

### MEASURING UP
Cut two squares of fabric to the width and depth of the pillow form, plus 1½in (4cm) all around. Lay one of the squares on the chair and mark the position of the uprights to which the pillow will be tied.

**1. Make the ties. You will need two** strips of fabric – one for each tie – 24in (60cm) by 2in (5cm). Fold each tie in half lengthwise, wrong sides together, and press. Fold each half of the strips in half again, so that the raw edges are enclosed, and press crisply.

**2. Open out both strips and fold in** ⅝in (1.5cm) at each end. Press. Refold the strips lengthwise and insert the hanging loop of a tassel at each end, pinning them in place. Sew down the length of each strip and across the turned-under ends. Press. Fold each tie in half crosswise and cut into two.

**3. Place a pair of ties at the penciled or** chalked positions on the right side of one of the fabric pillow pieces. The ties should point in toward the center of the fabric piece.

**▲ 4. Place the second fabric piece on** top, right sides facing, and sew together with a ⅝in (1.5cm) seam allowance. Leave an opening at the back between the two pairs of ties. Turn the fabric right side out and press.

**5. Sew a line of zig-zag stitching all** around the cushion, ½in (12mm) in from the edge. Zig-zag across the tasseled edge of each tie to secure them firmly. Put the pillow form inside and slip-stitch the opening together. Tie the pillow in place on the chair seat.

# MEDIEVAL

*Choose rich fabrics, such as velvets and tapestries, in dark hues.*

*Use trimmings to add glints of jewel colors — forest greens, ruby red,*

*midnight blue, deep russet — and brilliant flashes of gold.*

# tapestry drapes

*The sumptuous texture of this tapestry fabric is further enhanced by dramatic fringes whose weight helps the heavy curtain to hang evenly. The brass clips are a perfect foil to the variety of textures. Loop the curtain back with a rope and tassel tie-back and allow the fringes on the lower hem to spread attractively across the floor. This look, while not difficult to produce, will take a little more time than some projects, especially if you decide to make the fringes yourself.*

## MATERIALS

◆ Fabric

◆ Lining, if required

◆ Fringing

◆ Brass clips

◆ Rope and tassels

MEASURING UP

Each curtain should be the width of the pole plus half again. Add extra length so that the bottom of the curtain breaks on the floor and another 4in (10cm) for top and bottom hems. The measurements for the lining, if required, are the same, less 2in (5cm) on the width and 3in (7.5cm) on the length. Decide on the depth of the top overhang and add twice this measurement to the length of the main fabric only.

**I. Note that when cutting out a thick** fabric, such as tapestry or deep-pile velvet, the pile should always face up. Great care should also be taken when pressing such fabrics; a special velvet board can be used for the purpose.

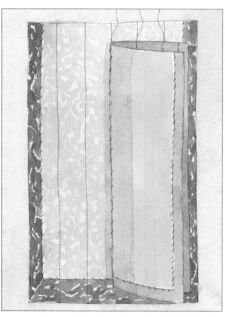

**▲ 2. Turn the sides and bottom hem of** the curtain by 2in (5cm) to the wrong side. Press. Miter the corners and stitch the hems in place. If lining the curtain, attach it in the same way as for the Golden Drapes on page 26. Turn the top hem by 2in (5cm) and press. Fold the overhang in half so that the pressed edge of the fabric just covers the top of the lining, then sew and press.

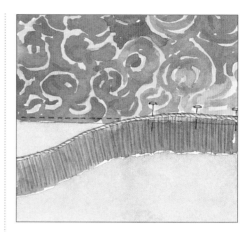

**▲ 3. Attach the fringing to the top and** bottom of the curtains. Pin the fringing braid in place, then baste and sew by hand. Turn in the edges to neaten.

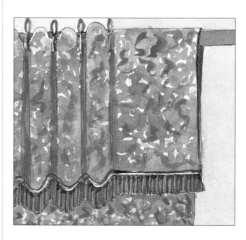

**▲ 4. Fold over the top of the curtain** so that an even amount of fabric falls to the front. Attach the brass clips to the folded edge, distributing them evenly.

# fleur-de-lys tie-back

*There are many interesting ways to hold back a pair of curtains. This stylish tie-back uses stunning gold braid and red tassels.*

## MATERIALS

◆ Fabric

◆ Braid

◆ Light padding

◆ Tassels

◆ Brass rings

## MEASURING UP

Hold a tape measure around the curtain at the desired height to give an idea of the length of the tie. Decide on the size of the decorative end band and subtract this from the length. The width should be 5in (13cm). Add ⅝in (1.5cm) all around for seam allowances.

**1. Cut two rectangles of fabric for the** main section of the tie-back. Cut one piece of padding without the seam allowance. Place the padding on the wrong side of one of the fabric pieces and slip-stitch in place around its outer edge to hold it in position. Place the two fabric pieces right sides together and stitch along both long edges. Turn right side out.

▲ **2. Cut two strips of braid to the** same length as the rectangle and stitch one along both long edges of the tie-back. Turn in the raw ends at one end to neaten and stitch in place.

**3. Cut two fabric rectangles for the** outer band. Sandwich the ends of three tassels between them at one end, right sides facing one another, and sew across this end to hold the tassels in place. Turn right side out and press.

▲ **4. Lay the tasseled band against the** main fabric, right sides facing and raw edges aligned, and sew. Turn under the seam allowance along the two side edges, and slip-stitch in place. Press. Fold the band over to enclose the raw edge of the main rectangle and slip-stitch in place. Press.

**5. Sew a strip of wide braid around this** outer band. Fold the tie-back in half and sew a brass ring at each end. Attach this to a hook on the wall.

# padded tie-back

*This thick, textural tie-back looks wonderful with rich fabrics, and allows you to mix two or three different materials, thus making a tie-back which relates to other fabrics in the room.*

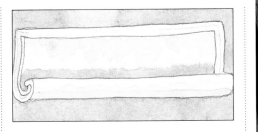

▲ **2. Lay the padding onto the lining,** aligning one long edge. Roll the two together and slip-stitch along the length. Sew across the ends.

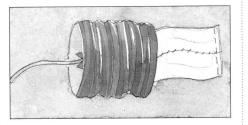

▲ **3. Fold the main fabric strips in half** lengthwise, right sides facing, and sew, using a seam allowance of ⅝in (1.5cm). Turn right side out. Pull the strips of padded lining through the fabric tubes using a strong thread attached to one end of the lining tubes. Stitch the three strips together at one end. Braid them and sew the ends to secure. Check the length.

**4. Finish the two ends with a 4in** (10cm) square of fabric. Fold the square in half, wrong sides facing one another. Lay the braid end inside the square. Fold in all raw edges of the square by ⅝in (1.5cm) to neaten and slip-stitch in place. Press.

**5. Sew a brass ring to the center of** each end. Thread through two cords, following the pattern of the braiding. Sew a tassel to the ends of the cords, one at each end of the tie-back.

## MATERIALS

◆ Fabric in three contrasting colors
◆ Lining
◆ Light padding
◆ Cord
◆ Tassels
◆ Brass rings

## MEASURING UP

Loop a tape measure loosely around the curtain at the desired height and hold the ends together against the wall. This will be the finished length of the tie-back.

**I. Cut three strips of fabric,** each 4in (10cm) wide by 1½ times the required finished length. Cut three strips of lining, 6in (15cm) wide by the same length as the fabric. Cut three strips of padding, 4½in (12cm) wide and 1in (2cm) shorter than the fabric.

# scalloped canopy

*This type of bed treatment will work well in situations that are either rather formal or perhaps too cramped for full drapes. The shape of the hanging pieces can be adapted to individual tastes and can also be trimmed with bobbles or tassels. This style can be stapled directly onto wood or adapted to suit a metal rail.*

## MATERIALS

◆ Fabric
◆ Interfacing
◆ Braid
◆ Hooks and rings (optional)

MEASURING UP

Cut two strips of fabric for each rail. Each strip should be the length of the rail and the desired depth, plus seam allowances all around of ⅝in (1.5cm). Cut a strip of interfacing without the allowances for each rail. For the hanging shapes, start by cutting out shapes in paper and taping them in place in order to determine proportions. Cut two templates in paper or card, one without allowances for the interfacing and one adding ⅝in (1.5cm) all around for the fabric. Each shape will require one piece of interfacing and two pieces of fabric.

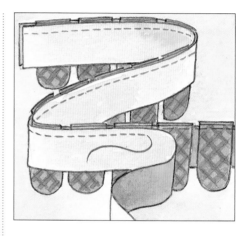

▲ **2. Lay one of the strips out flat,** right side up. Distribute the shaped pieces evenly along the length of the strip and tack in position. Lay a second strip on top, right sides facing, and sew along the top edge, making sure that all of the shaped pieces are firmly caught in. Sew down the width of the strip and tie off the ends of the stitching.

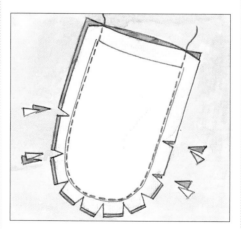

▲ **1. Press a piece of interfacing to the** wrong side of one of the fabric shapes. Put the fabric pieces together, right sides facing, and sew all around except for the top. Trim the seams and clip the corners. Turn right side out and press crisply. Repeat as many times as necessary.

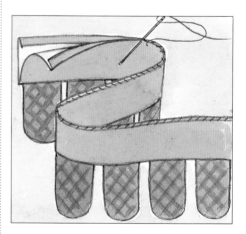

▲ **3. Trim the seams and clip the** corners. Turn right side out. Turn the allowances in on the long open end and slip-stitch or top-stitch closed. Press crisply. Sew on trimmings or braid as desired. Staple the long strip to the wood of the bed canopy. Alternatively, hand sew curtain hooks to the inside of the strip, distributing them evenly. (Heading tape will show.) Hang from curtain hooks.

# studded wallhanging

*Give walls a feeling of richness with fabric wallhangings. The chosen fabric can link with the colors and style of the rest of the room and also provide extra insulation. A single piece of fabric can be used behind a bedhead, or you could cover all the walls in a lightweight version. White muslin with big brass studs would look just as marvelous as this example.*

## MATERIALS

◆ Fabric

◆ Metal studs or wooden pegs

## MEASURING UP

Decide on the area of wall you wish to cover. Add extra fabric to the width to allow it to drape between the studs. Add 1¼in (3cm) at the sides for seam allowances. Decide on the number of studs/pegs you require and cut the appropriate number of ties. Each tie measures 16in (40cm) by 4in (10cm), plus ⅝in (1.5cm) for seams.

**1. Neaten the sides of the wallhanging** by turning ⅝in (1.5cm) over to the wrong side. Press. Turn by the same amount again, sew and press. Turn over both top and bottom hems by 1½in (4cm). Press. Turn over by the same amount again, sew and press.

**2. Make the ties by folding each strip** in half lengthwise, right sides together. Sew down the length ⅝in (1.5cm) in from the edge, leaving a gap of 2in (5cm) in the center. Sew across both ends.

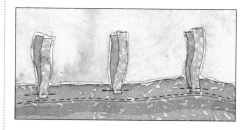

▲ **3. Turn the ties right side out** through the gap. Press. Fold the ties in half widthwise and pin them at the fold to the top hem of the wallhanging. Each tie should be positioned ⅝in (1.5cm) from the top edge. Sew them in place.

▲ **4. Position the decorative studs or** pegs on the wall. Knot the ties around them and adjust the drape as required.

# ruched bell-pull

*You can easily enhance an old or rather dull bell-pull by giving it this simple but attractive treatment. You can use wide braid or ribbon, or a strip of fabric that echoes your room's color scheme.*

## MATERIALS
◆ Tassel and cord
◆ Fabric or braid

## MEASURING UP
Decide on the length of the bell-pull and cut the cord to this length, plus 8in (20cm) for knotting. Cut a strip of fabric or braid twice the length and wide enough to fit around the cord plus ½in (12mm) for seam allowances.

**1. Use a tassel and cord that are pre-attached if possible. If not, sew the tassel firmly to the end of the length of cord. Use strong quilting thread as it must withstand being pulled.**

**▲ 2. Fold the strip of fabric or braid in half lengthwise and sew down the edge, using a seam allowance of ⅜in (1cm). Turn under a small hem at each end and sew to neaten. Turn the tube right side out and then pull it over the rope. Allow the fabric to ruche together.**

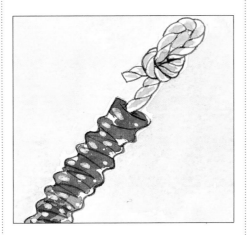

**▲ 3. Make a loop at the free end of the cord and tie a knot. This can be used to attach the pull to the bell mechanism. Seal the raw end of the cord to prevent it from fraying.**

# coordinated trimmings

*This is an example of how to coordinate a broad mix of fabrics and colors with a trimmings treatment. The natural linen tassels and braids are used to produce a less formal look than that of gold trimmings.*

### MATERIALS

◆ Ready-made curtains

◆ Ready-made pillows

◆ Cord, fringing and tassels

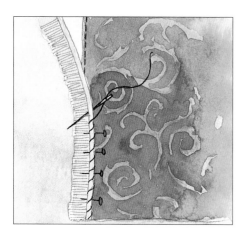

▲ **I. It is important to find a really** nice range of coordinating accessories. These can be sewn onto the edges of seams or hems either by hand or machine. Always pin and tack beforehand and keep a smooth, continuous line when sewing. Trim the cord ends with tassels to neaten.

# tufts and tassels

*You can make these attractive woolly tufts while watching television or chatting to a friend! Distribute them over your pillow either at random or in a regular, symmetrical pattern.*

## MATERIALS

◆ Square pillow
◆ Knitting yarn in either a matching or contrasting color
◆ Tassel board
◆ Cord and tassels

## MEASURING UP

The size of the tufts and the quantity required varies depending on the size of the pillow to be decorated. Experiment by moving the pegs on the tassel board and trying different sizes of tuft. Experiment also with the amount and thickness of the knitting yarn as this will result in thinner or fatter tufts.

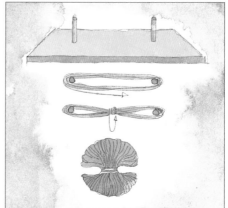

▲ 1. Wrap a loop of yarn around the two pegs on the tassel board and tie to secure. Continue wrapping the yarn around the pegs until the desired size is achieved. Make sure that the original knot is hidden. Wrap the end of the yarn around the middle of the loop tightly and tie-off.

2. Remove the tuft from the pegs. Dip the wrapped center into boiling water to shrink it. Dry with a hair dryer or use an automatic clothes dryer if making a large quantity. Mark the positions for the tufts on the pillow with pins.

▲ 3. Sew braid around the edge of the pillow. Sew the tufts by hand at the marked positions. Lay a length of cord along each line of tufts, wrapping the cord around the center of each one. Stitch the cord in place and sew a tassel at each end at the side seam of the pillow.

*Choose checked prints, opulent*

*plaids and bold trimmings in rich, strong colors.*

*Teamed with the warm textures of woolen weaves and*

*woven cottons, the results will be stunning.*

# TARTANS
# & CHECKS

# plaid and muslin curtain

*Curtains in a lightweight fabric, such as muslin or a polycotton mix, can make attractive under-curtains or can be used on their own. They look best in generous swathes with a dramatic contrasting top band. A tassel fringing or pom-pom braid complete the look.*

## MATERIALS

◆ Lightweight muslin or similar fabric

◆ Contrasting fabric for top band

◆ Iron-on interfacing

◆ Tassel fringing

CURTAIN – MEASURING UP

The main fabric width should be that of the pole, plus any additional width required. Add an extra 6in (15cm) to the length for hems. The top band should be the width of the curtain, plus 1½in (4cm) for turnings, by a depth of 14in (36cm) including allowances. The fringing should be the width of the curtain, plus ½in (1.5cm) either end to turn in.

**1. Hem the sides of the curtain by** turning ⅝in (1.5cm) to the wrong side and press. Repeat, sew and press again. Turn up the bottom hem by 2in (5cm) and press. Repeat, sew and press again.

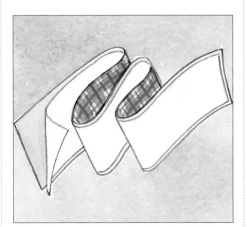

▲ **2. Cut a strip of interfacing and** fuse it to the wrong side of the top band fabric. Fold the top band in half lengthwise and press. Place it along the top edge of the main fabric, with the right side of the band on the wrong side of the fabric.

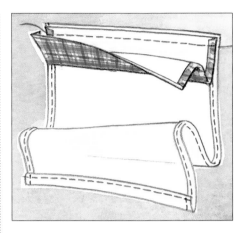

▲ **3. Sew along the top edge, using a** seam allowance of 2in (5cm). Turn in the sides and bottom of the band by 1in (2.5cm) and press. Turn the top band over to the front of the curtain so that the raw edges are enclosed. Press and top-stitch in place.

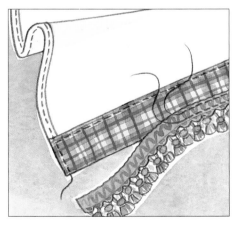

▲ **4. Pin the tassel fringing across the** folded edge of the top band, turning in the ends to neaten. Sew in place. Attach hooks evenly across the top of the main fabric of the curtain and hang in place so that the top band falls forward.